MW00768640

Developing a Successful Softball Program

Mike Noel
Stephenie Jordan

©2004 Coaches Choice. All rights reserved. Printed in the United States.

No part of this book may be reproduced, stored in a retrieval system, or transmitted, in any form or by any means, electronic, mechanical, photocopying, recording, or otherwise, without the prior permission of Coaches Choice.

ISBN: 1-58518-877-8
Library of Congress Control Number: 2003116001
Book layout: Jeanne Hamilton
Cover design: Jeanne Hamilton
Front cover photo: Leslie Scott
Diagrams: Stephenie Jordan
Text photos: Chapters 3 and 4 — David Menendian

Coaches Choice
P.O. Box 1828
Monterey, CA 93942
www.coacheschoice.com

Acknowledgments

With sincere thanks and appreciation to my Lord and Savior, Jesus Christ; my husband, Jody; my parents, Roger and Claire Scott; to the first-ever Garrison High School softball team; and to our children, Scott and Rebekah, who are the greatest joy and blessing in our lives.

– Stephenie Jordan

I want to thank all the players (past and present), coaches, and administrators at Clovis High School for the opportunities and memories you have provided me throughout my career. To Stephenie Jordan, thanks for all your direction and guidance. To all the great coaches I've had in my life: Tony Petersen, Max Newberry, Stan Bledsoe, Bob Bennett, and Tim Painton. To Tim Douglas, thanks for everything you do for Cougar Softball. To my wonderful wife, Tiffany, and my daughter, Avery, thank you for all your love and support. To my mom and sister, Carleen and Michelle Noel, I love you both. And to my father, Don, I miss you.

– Mike Noel

Foreword

During both my days as a player and my career as a coach, I have always been acutely aware of the importance of quality instructional and teaching resources. As such, *Developing a Successful Softball Program* is a much-needed addition to every coach's library. Coaches who care about providing a positive experience for their players and staff members will benefit from the information provided in this well-written, comprehensive book. The book is a terrific tool for coaches (particularly new coaches) who want to have a well-designed, well-run program. Appropriate for coaches at all competitive levels, the book offers an easy-to-follow handbook for softball coaches concerning what to do and when to do it to put together a successful program.

By its inherent nature, athletics is structured so that winning is the goal. Coaches who care about their sport, however, understand that winning is not their only goal. A number of factors (some beyond the control of the coach) determine the ultimate outcome of a game. Arguably, a more important and realistic objective for coaches is to do everything in their power to put their team in a position to win. UCLA's renowned coach John Wooden referred to this focal point as "competitive greatness." Mike Noel and Stephenie Jordan's book can help every coach in this regard. Theirs is an exceptional book for those coaches who don't want to leave anything to chance.

Sue Enquist
Head Softball Coach
UCLA

Preface

Developing a Successful Softball Program is a resource-packed, comprehensive handbook that touches on more than the X's and O's of the sport. Many areas left untouched by other softball books are covered here, including tryout procedures, job descriptions for your assistants, game day considerations, and much more.

Chapter 1 is a season timeline that highlights important aspects that need to be addressed before and during the season. The next two chapters will give you insight into planning the season and having tryouts, the components of a good practice, drills for each skill, and sample practice schedules. Chapters 4 through 6 are related specifically to the X's and O's of coaching softball and include coaching strategies for each fundamental skill, details on how to organize your line-up, strategies for hitting, bunting, stealing, and defending the first-and-third situation, and much more. The scouting chapter includes charts, forms, and questions to ask when evaluating your opponent. Chapter 8 is dedicated to game day considerations, including what to take to an away game, how to prepare your field, keeping stats during the game, and how to deal with the media. Chapter 9 summarizes season-ending responsibilities and program management, which wouldn't be complete without dealing with an off-season program. Chapter 10 explains how to plan your off-season, activities to use during a practice, a rating system for the athletes, a sample 10-week program, and a summer workout program.

Finally, the appendices provide detailed information about planning your own tournament, field maintenance, and fundraising. These sections are presented in a timeline format and take you from the planning stages to the day of the event and after.

Developing a Successful Softball Program is intended for use as a reference. Pick and choose what you need when you need it. We hope you find it gives you the added edge you need to be a successful coach.

Contents

Photo: Leslie Scott

A Brief History of Softball

Softball was invented in 1887 when some Yale and Harvard alumni began using a boxing glove and a broomstick to play a game of baseball. George Hancock, a reporter for the Chicago Board of Trade, used the laces of the boxing glove to tie it into a ball and realized the large, soft ball did not travel nearly as far as a baseball. Hancock called his game "indoor baseball" and it became very popular in the Chicago area. Eventually, the game was moved outside, but played on a much smaller field than the traditional baseball field. By 1926, the game was officially named "softball" and it was further promoted during a 55-team tournament at the 1933 World's Fair held in Chicago. Today, thousands of players of all ages play in hundreds of softball leagues. Fast-pitch softball is the most competitive version of the game, especially for high school and college-age women, while slow-pitch is a popular recreational game for any age.

1

Season Planning Timeline

September

- Send letters to athletes
- Develop (or update) team standards and expectations
- Meet with prospective team members
- Schedule the season
- Check the fund balance
- Schedule college trip or clinic
- Order booster material
- Inventory equipment
- Make a needs and wants list for the athletic director
- Request field improvements
- Join coaching organizations
- Check varsity players' schedules

Sending Letters to Athletes

Because your sport is in the spring, you'll want to keep in contact with your athletes throughout the fall and winter. An effective and easy way to communicate is with letters. The letters could include any information and important dates before the first day of practice. Also include congratulations to those excelling in other sports or in the classroom. Figure 1.1 illustrates an example of a letter that could be sent to prospective players.

Send a welcome back letter to your returning players with a quick note at the beginning of school. Include reminders to them about their commitment to classwork, to keeping in shape, etc.

Developing (or Updating) Team Standards and Expectations

The athletic director will probably have guidelines for the entire athletic program. You will certainly have to

Dear Prospective Softball Player,

I hope this letter finds your fall semester going well. The following list includes some important information about meetings, practice times, and other dates of interest.

DATE	EVENT	LOCATION	TIME
Sept. 15	Physicals	Field House	3:00 - 6:00 pm
Jan. 6	Tryouts	Softball Field	3:00 - 5:00 pm
Jan. 9	Parent meeting	Cafeteria	7:00 pm
Jan. 12	First day of practice	Softball Field	3:30 - 5:30 pm
Feb. 10	Media Day	Softball Field	3:00 pm
Feb. 17	Meet the Lady _____ Intersquad Scrimmage	Softball Field	5:30 pm
Feb. 25	Scrimmage vs. TBA	There	5:00 pm

Hope you had a great summer! I look forward to seeing you on Sept. 15th.

Sincerely,

Coach Noel

Figure 1.1. Letter to players

adhere to those policies, but if you are given the liberty to create your own, consider the following general fundamental areas that may need clarification, and address them to fit your personal situation:

- Classroom expectations
- Alcohol and drug violations
- Stealing
- Lettering
- Travel to and from games
- Attendance
- Excused and unexcused absences
- Profanity
- Quitting the team
- Injury or illness
- Unsportsmanlike conduct
- Dress code
- Equipment management
- Multiple extracurricular athletes
- Use of technology (cell phones, headphones, etc.)
- Suspension from school
- Disrespect to teachers and coaches
- Locker room behavior
- Demerit system

Demerit System

The demerit system can be very useful for an athletic program. Assign point values for violations of the team policies and time-based point totals for further disciplinary action. For example, once an athlete receives five points (or demerits), the athlete incurs a one-game suspension. However, if an athlete goes one week without getting any points, one point is deducted from her total. If the athlete accumulates 15 points during the season, she is suspended from the team. Some examples of how points may be assigned include:

- Suspension from school = five points
- Cheating or any other academic dishonesty = four points
- Unexcused absence from practice = three points
- Unexcused absence from leadership council meeting = three points
- Unexcused absence from class = three points
- Unexcused absence from tutorials = two points
- Dress code violations = one point
- Dressing room violations = one point
- Failure to follow instructions = one point
- Other = (up to the discretion of the coach)

Commitment Page

The last page of your policies should be a summary of what you expect. Include a line for the athlete's signature and the signature of the athlete's parents, as illustrated in Figure 1.2.

THE COMMITMENT TO EXCELLENCE

I have read the handbook and understand the policies of the softball program and the athletic program.

In addition to keeping the aforementioned policies, I will:

Follow all school rules, district rules, and UIL rules;

Strive to excel academically;

Not lie or steal;

Not use alcohol, illegal drugs, tobacco, or other harmful substances; and,

Give my best effort at all times.

I hereby state that I have received, read, and understand the policies and agree to abide by these policies in all respects.

Student signature: _____

Parent/Guardian signature: _____

Date: _____

Figure 1.2. Commitment page

The Clovis Softball System

We operate on the principle that each of us is responsible to find the answer to success. The loser stops with the problem....The winner seeks the answer to that problem.

You can expect loyalty from the coaching staff. The coaching staff must insist upon loyalty in return.

"Practices afford a daily opportunity for players to make positive statements about themselves on the field and to demonstrate the quality of player they aspire to become. We want our players to be aware of the personal practice legacy they will be remembered for at Clovis High. We realize that some players, due to greater levels of experience, skill development, and maturity will be better game performers than others. But every player on the team can be a great practice player while striving to become a gamer.

Earning peer respect in practice is vital to the team's success. The staff and players need to understand and agree that practices are characterized by a high level of intensity and game-level enthusiasm. Your coaching staff will be challenging players to maximize their physical, mental, intellectual, and emotional performance. We often conduct teaching with a great deal of pressure that calls for game-situation performance."*

In order to attain real success we must trust in each other. The coaching staff must make certain decisions. Team members don't have to agree with these decisions, but they must honor and trust these decisions. We trust that you will abide by the following rules:

1. Be on time. Practice will begin at 3:15 p.m., unless otherwise notified.
2. Missed practices, without prior arrangements, will not be tolerated.
3. Hustle is the key to our success. Be committed to this in practice as well as games.
4. "Second guessing" or derogatory remarks made by the members of this team to anyone other than the coaching staff will be dealt with severely.

* From *Baseball Coaches Bible*

5. As a member of the Clovis High School Softball team, you are representing this program. This means off the field as well as on. Representation includes such things as:
   a. Pictures and interviews.
   b. Conduct during playing of the National Anthem prior to a game.
   c. Conduct in the classroom.
   d. Conduct in the community.
6. Poise is essential to superior performance. Helmet and bat throwing, use of profanity and / or temper tantrums do not display poise. They will not be tolerated.
7. Use of alcohol, tobacco, or narcotics will result in appropriate disciplinary action.
8. We feel that appearance is important. The following standards must be met:
   a. Neat and well groomed in uniform. (clean shoes, clean socks, etc.)
   b. Appropriate uniform. No deviations
   c. Dress code will be severely enforced.
9. Maintaining academic standards is a must. Those who fall behind in their classes will be attending Study Hall.
10. These rules are in effect during your participation in the program and do not end until your completion in the program.
11. Sportsmanship is important, as is loyalty to school, staff, and team members.
12. You should show respect for officials at all times.
13. You should show modesty in victory, graciousness in defeat, and pride in our effort.
14. We will be a class organization.

The glory and publicity you are receiving is due to your team membership; therefore, you are required to represent the program, not your own individual philosophy.

Because you are a member of this program, you are closely observed by many people. With this in mind, it is important to maintain the highest standards in all aspects of young adult life.

Figure 1.3. Sample standards and expectations statement

Figure 1.3 gives an example of a team standards and expectations statement.

Meeting with Prospective Team Members

Pass out the program handbook and go over each item in detail. Among the items the handbook should include are the following:

- School history – Include team records, individual records, names of players who went on to play collegiate ball, and former award winners.

- Season schedule

- Maps to schools for out-of-town games (www.mapquest.com is a good place to start)

- School requirements for participation

- Team rules and policies

- Information on equipment – For example, what is issued by the school and what the athlete should provide.

- Criteria for earning a varsity letter

- Phone numbers and e-mail of school, coaching staff, and teammates – Also make a laminated, wallet-sized card with everyone's number on it for players to keep in their wallets.

- Academic expectations – Have your athletes set a goal for a specific GPA they would like to achieve. Also, have them list their course schedule and pinpoint any courses that might be considered "problem courses." A sample questionnaire is illustrated in Figure 1.4.

```
CLOVIS HIGH SOFTBALL
Player Questionnaire

Name: _____ Grade: _____
Address: _____ City: _____
Zip: _____ Telephone: _____
Counselor: _____

Guardian's Names:
Name: _____ Relation: _____
Name: _____ Relation: _____

Brothers and Sisters and their ages:
_____
_____
_____

Class Schedule:
Period   Subject                    Teacher    Room#
  0      _____
  1      _____
  2      _____
  3      _____
  4      _____
  5      _____
  6      _____
  7      _____

What level do you plan on playing (frosh, JV, var): _____
What positions do you play: _____
What team do you play for in the summer: _____
What other sports do you play at CHS: _____
Born (date and city): _____
Shoe size (men/women): _____ T-shirt size: _____
```

Biggest sports thrill: _____
_____
_____

Career plans/goals: _____
_____
_____

Few people know this about me: _____
_____

Hobbies: _____
_____

School activities (govt., clubs, etc): _____
_____

Hero/Role Model (and why): _____

Height: _____

Awards won at Clovis High (athletic or academic): _____
_____

Favorite movie: _____

Favorite food: _____

Favorite TV show: _____

Write a paragraph describing what you like about Clovis Softball:

Figure 1.4. Academic expectations questionnarie

- Practice rules

  ❑ Always be on time to practice and get dressed quickly.

  ❑ The training room is never an excuse for being late. Get there as early as necessary so you can be on the field in a timely manner.

  ❑ Wear the appropriate practice gear unless otherwise instructed.

  ❑ Do not wear jewelry during practice time.

  ❑ Be detail-oriented. Learn the drill and the name of the drill. Ask questions if you do not fully understand…but listen! Do not ask questions just to be asking questions.

  ❑ Accept criticism as constructive. No criticism is personal or meant for embarrassment. The coaches are trying to help you become the best player possible.

  ❑ Be helpful to your teammates. Softball is a team game and we can only win as a team. You are expected to compete against your teammates every day to help each player reach her potential.

  ❑ Look your coaches in the eyes during instructions. "Listen" with your eyes.

  ❑ Do not argue with your teammates, coaches, etc. at any time.

  ❑ Respect your coaches and teammates and earn their respect as well.

- Hustle from one drill to another and shag balls if necessary.
- Use appropriate language and address your teammates and coaches with respect at all times.
- Strive to work to your fullest potential during practice time; eliminate wasted time.
- Leave all problems out of the locker room; certainly do not take them to the field.
- Do not gossip or plan social events during practice.
- Be intense and enthusiastic about each day of practice. Practice is what makes the difference in your ability to succeed.

- "Cougar" capsule – Have player's fill out a general information sheet to be passed out to fans during home games. Highlight one player during each home game. If you have a short season, highlight more than one. Have players fill in the following information:
  - Nickname
  - Favorite food
  - Favorite music artist(s)
  - Favorite sports team
  - Favorite place to hang out
  - Favorite book
  - Favorite class
  - Favorite hobby
  - Favorite video game
  - Favorite movie
  - Favorite TV show
  - Favorite athlete
  - Favorite non-softball activity
  - One word that describes you

- If you were going on a road trip and could only take one CD, which one would you take?
- Best vacation or trip you have ever taken
- Opponent you would most like to beat
- If you could play another sport, what would it be?
- Best thing about being a student-athlete
- Best part about your game
- What is the best sporting event you have ever attended as a spectator?

Scheduling the Season

If you have an experienced team, find tougher opponents for your pre-district/pre-conference play. Playing top-level teams can give your team the confidence to say, "No one in our district is better than (whoever), but we played with them." On the other hand, if your team is struggling or young, find some weaker teams or teams with equal ability to build some confidence as you approach district or conference play. Remember to designate one game for parents' night and another for introducing Diamond Club members (preferably at games where you need extra support). Once you have your schedule in place, print a clean copy and distribute it to everyone who needs it (players, principals, umpire assignor, athletic director, etc.).

Checking the Fund Balance

See where you stand at the beginning of the season so you know how much money you have to work with. The amount in your budget will also dictate how many fundraisers (if any) you will need to plan.

Scheduling a College Trip or Clinic

Contact a successful college coach and arrange to go watch a practice and then spend some time visiting with the coach afterwards. Try to attend at least one clinic a year as well.

Ordering Booster Material

Having team shirts, sweatshirts, hats, and other items with your team logo is a great way to promote your team and the sport they play. Sell the apparel at all home games, as well as other team functions. The team logo items also make great gifts for administration, people who donate their time or supplies to your field or program, or other support staff. What you have printed on the shirts could correlate with the motivational theme you've chosen, or you might purchase ready-made shirts. Have pencils made in team colors with your logo on them. They make great little gifts that you can send with letters to your players.

Inventorying Equipment

To develop a list of needs and wants, you'll need to know what you've got. If you are new on the job, don't rely on the list left by the previous coach. Figure 1.5 illustrates a sample form that can be used to record the equipment.

Making a Needs and Wants List for the Athletic Director

If you want some items that may be out of the ordinary, then do what you can to make a professional presentation to your athletic director. For example, if you think you can't live without a

Anywhere Independent School District Women's Softball Inventory 2004-2005					
Item Description	New	Usable	Old	Total	Needed

Figure 1.5. Inventory sheet

specific pitching machine, then find three companies that produce them, find the best price, and show you've done your homework. If the athletic director rejects the idea, then begin thinking about a fundraiser (see Appendix C). Among the items you should include in your needs list are the following:

❑ Annually

Shoes – Order new shoes for your squads. A common game shoe goes a long way to help a group feel more like a team.

Softballs – Depending on the number of games you'll be playing, 5 to 10 dozen softballs will do. Use last season's softballs for soft toss and other hitting drills.

Bats – Although the players often have their own bats, buy two bats (33" and 34") per season. Base the purchase on technology rather than price. If a bat exists that's going to give you a couple more hits per game, get it.

Protective equipment –Your catchers and hitters must be well-protected. Get your catchers the best and most comfortable equipment you can find. Make sure you have enough helmets of each size so that players are not wearing the wrong-size helmet at the plate.

Scorebooks – One per season per team is sufficient.

Socks/Stirrups – Depending on your preference, you can choose ribbon stirrups, two-in-one socks, or a team-color sock.

Bathrooms – If your facilities do not have on-site bathrooms, contact a local waste company to order some bathrooms (a.k.a. Port-o-potties) for use at home games. Two (one each for males and females) should be enough. Order more if you make the playoffs.

Chalk and paint – Check with your athletic director to find out how much you will need to purchase. Chalk and paint may be bought in bulk when the head football coach, head baseball coach, or field maintenance director orders, so you may be able to pick some up from one of them as you need it.

Chalker – If you have enough funds, consider purchasing one of your own. If not, you could probably share with the baseball program.

Cups and coolers – Make sure you have plenty of cups for an entire season and at least two coolers.

Athletic training supplies – The only two words you need to know about 90% of the injuries you'll see are "ice it." Hopefully, you will have a trainer on staff that can deal with serious knee problems or severe strains and pulls. Otherwise, learn how to tape an ankle. Among the items that you should consider ordering for your travel kit are the following:

Adhesive tape

Pre-wrap material

Bandages/Band-Aids (assorted sizes)

Butterfly strips

Contact solution

Elastic knee sleeves (S, M, & L)

Elastic thigh sleeves (S, M, & L)

Eyewash

Feminine napkins

Gauze (1-inch and 2-inch rolls)

Heel cups (plastic)

Instant cold packs

Internal agents (Tylenol, ibuprofen, aspirin)

Peroxide

Safety pins

Scissors

Sterile pads (2 x 2's and 3 x 3's)

Tape adherent (spray can)

Tape cutters

Tweezers

❑ As needed

Uniforms – Dress your team in the best possible uniforms you can afford. The better quality you buy, the longer they will last. Make sure you have enough to fit everyone—not just clothe everyone. Some girls may not fit perfectly into those 1997 uniforms your teams are still wearing. You want your team to look good and feel comfortable.

Practice uniforms – Issue these the first day you meet and require that everyone wear them. When everyone dresses the same, you have a sense of team.

Pitching machines – Pitching machines can be very useful. They can be used not only for batting practice, but also for bunting drills, catching drills, and other defensive drills.

Protective nets – Use nets to protect a pitcher or feeder during batting practice. They can also be used for batting drills, for example, to hit into during soft toss drills. They can also be used for protection for defensive players during batting practice. For example, if you wanted to hit ground balls with throws to first base to your shortstop, you could protect the first baseman from a batted ball.

Player bags and jackets – Both bags and jackets help add to the team concept, as well as serve useful purposes to a softball player. Buy them in team colors and purchase the best you can afford.

Ball bags – Try to order two ball bags for travel: one bag for softballs and one for whiffle balls.

Bases and pitching rubber – Replace these as needed.

Fungo bats – You should have one per coach.

Hitting tees – Three tees is all you'll need.

Fielding paddles – Order one fielding paddle per infielder if your budget allows.

Training bat –Also known as a thunderstick, a training bat is a thin, one-inch bat that can be used for bunting drills.

Little league bat – Purchase a small, lightweight little league bat for one-handed hitting drills.

Video equipment – You'll need a camera, a good VCR, and plenty of tapes. Video can be a valuable tool for teaching skills and mechanics.

Requesting Field Improvements

Providing an enjoyable place for softball should be a priority. Try to make one or two improvements each year to your field. Additions to your field could include:

- Flag pole
- Foul poles
- Sound system with speakers
- Enclosed dugouts
- Fence cap
- Bullpens
- Wind screen or other backing for outfield fence
- Signage (championship titles, retired numbers, fence distances, field name, slogans, etc.)
- Scoreboard
- Hitting tunnels
- Trees (behind the outfield fence or surrounding the field's perimeter)
- Bat/helmet racks
- Extra bleachers
- Field cart (used for dragging the skinned area of the field)

Joining Coaching Organizations

Join the National Fastpitch Coaches Association (www.nfca.org), as well as your state coaches association. Membership in these organizations allows you to nominate your players for all-region, All-American, and academic All-American status. You will also get a monthly newsletter that contains drills, instruction, and clinic dates. The dues paid to be a member of the organization sometimes include admission to their convention, where you can hear notable speakers, get informed of rule changes, and browse the products sold by a variety of vendors.

Checking Varsity Players' Schedules

If you travel a great distance to away games, you might consider moving all of your varsity players into a non-academic class (e.g. PE) during the last period of the day.

October

- Fill out purchase order forms
- Order equipment
- Fill out travel paperwork and requests
- Arrange for substitutes for clinics/trips
- Get an academic plan ready
- Secure coaching positions

Filling Out Purchase Order Forms

If your business office doesn't already have a purchase order form that it employs, Figure 1.6 offers an example of a form that you could use.

Ordering Equipment

When ordering equipment, write down the representative's name, phone number, and the date and time of your order, so you will know who to

PURCHASE REQUEST FORM					
Date: Requested By: Approved By: Purchase Order #:					
Quantity	Catalogue #	Description		Unit Price	Total
			REQUISITION TOTAL :		

Figure 1.6. Purchase order form

contact in case of an error. Make copies of the purchase order requests and compare invoices of shipped items with your list. Highlight items as they arrive.

Filling Out Travel Paperwork and Requests

Under normal circumstances, the transportation director at your school will insist on having at least three days' notice to provide transportation for your team. Get as many forms as you'll need for all of your out-of-town games and fill them all out at once. Before each trip, confirm with the director a few days in advance that your bus/van will be ready.

Arranging for Substitutes for Clinics/Trips

Alert the secretary in charge of getting substitutes as soon as you know the dates you will be gone for a trip or a clinic. Then verify that you have a substitute a few days before you leave.

Getting an Academic Plan Ready

Whether or not your state has a strict rule about passing classes before being eligible to play, teachers appreciate the interest you take in the academic success of your athletes. After all, without academics, extracurricular activities would not exist. Also, monitoring your players' grades from the start of the school year sends a message about what will be expected during your season in the spring. Grades are another way for players to strive for greatness. They give every player the opportunity to succeed. The following six-step procedure can be employed to monitor the academic progress of your athletes. If you have campus e-mail, these steps can be altered.

Step #1: Type a list of all participating athletes on one sheet, using columns and a smaller font if necessary (see Figure 1.7).

Step #2: Distribute the list of players to the teachers. Ask them to circle the names of any players they

---

Teacher's Name: _____

Teachers,

I would like to implement a weekly grade check for the softball players in order to ensure their academic success. As a coaching staff, we will work with you and help with discipline as well as tutoring, if necessary.

Please look over the following list, circle any softball players you have in class, add any that aren't on this list, and return it to Coach Noel's box by Friday afternoon. This will be the last time you will have to sort through the entire roster. You will have an individualized sheet starting Monday or Tuesday. Thanks for your help.

Mike Noel

Beard, Ramey	Noel, Avery	Talbert, Wegi
Beard, Vicki	Noel, Carleen	Vititow, Stacy
Beasley, Jeanette	Noel, Tiffany	Washburn, Kris
Beaver, Lannette	Norman, Ronda	Washburn, Sydney
Brooks, Barbara	Ortiz, Rebecca	Watson, Rhonda
Frazer, Judy	Peterson, Samantha	Weddle, Glenda
Jennings, Charise	Pierce, Kim	White, Norma
Jordan, Jean	Rolen, Stacy	Young, Brooke
Lopez, Sarah	Scott, Claire	Young, Denita
Lyle, Martha	Scott, Toni	Young, Taylor

Figure 1.7. Teacher's list

have in class and then return the form to you (or your box). Keep a master list of all teachers who have turned in their sheets and track down those who haven't.

Step #3: Once you have each teacher's list, type individual reports for each teacher listing only the athletes in that teacher's classes. Making the individual lists requires some work, but it makes it easier on the teachers. Figure 1.8 shows an example of a sample weekly grade report form.

Step #4: After the first grade check, compile all the information into one report and divide the number of athletes with academic or behavioral problems among your coaches. Each coach should speak directly to the teacher and work on improving the student's situation. Figure 1.9 shows a sample summary report form that can be used.

Step #5: Be sure to also keep up with the athletes that are doing well. Recognize honor roll students by posting a sign on their locker or on the bulletin board.

Step #6: Prepare a report to be presented to the school board during each grading period. Determine each player's grade point average for each team and

LADY TOUCAN WEEKLY GRADE REPORT

Teacher: Talbert, Grover
Week of: August 21-25th

Please check the list and make necessary changes (add or delete names). Then, complete the form and return it to Coach Jordan's box by Thursday morning. We would like to meet with you if you have a student-athlete who is failing (or nearly failing) or has been a discipline problem. Thanks for your support.

NAME	GRADE	BEHAVIOR	COMMENTS
Adair, Laurie	P F B	E S U	
Awalt, Mary	P F B	E S U	
Beard, Ramey	P F B	E S U	
Douglas, Juliet	P F B	E S U	
Jordan, Rebekah	P F B	E S U	
Noel, Avery	P F B	E S U	
Noel, Tiffany	P F B	E S U	
Peterson, Samantha	P F B	E S U	
	P F B	E S U	
	P F B	E S U	

KEY:
P - Passing
F - Failing
B - Borderline
E - Excellent
S - Satisfactory
U - Unsatisfactory

ADDITIONAL COMMENTS:

Figure 1.8. Weekly grade report form

GRADE REPORT FOR WEEK OF: August 21-25th				
Teacher's Name	Student's Name	Beh.	Gr.	Comments
Don Noel	Carleen Noel	S	P	Needs to make up a test.
Dave Bens	Lisa Peterson	E	P	Hasn't turned in two papers.
Tim Douglas	Vicki Beard	S	P	Has missed six days of class, but still has good grades.

Figure 1.9. Report summary

then present the following information: number of A's, B's, C's, D's, and F's; team GPAs; A honor roll members; A and B honor roll members; and incompletes. If you want to get fancy, graph this information using Excel. Include a cover sheet as well. Figure 1.10 illustrates an example of how this information can be organized and presented.

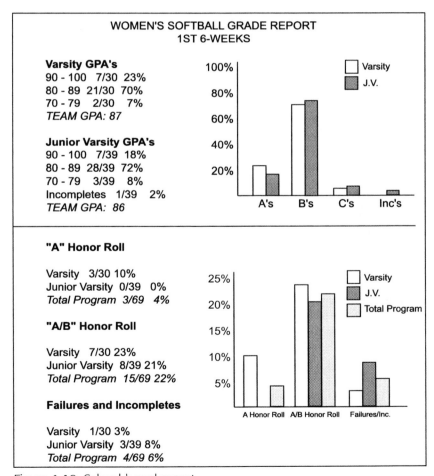

Figure 1.10. School board report

Securing Coaching Positions

If your state requires that only certified teachers who are employed by the school can coach, then the coaching positions will need to be arranged at the end of the previous school year. If your assistants are not employed by the school, get a commitment from them by at least the end of October.

November

- Send a letter to players
- Make a media guide
- Get inning sponsors

Sending a Letter to Players

Send a letter to let all athletes know when the winter workouts will begin. The winter workouts are open to anyone who intends to try out for the team in January. See Chapter 10 for a detailed approach to off-season workouts.

Making a Media Guide

The media guide can be as simple or elaborate as you like. Most football teams have them made and include pictures of all the players and coaches, a roster, and a schedule. Consider obtaining a media guide from a college nearby that highlights the softball team and use it as a template for your own media guide.

Getting Inning Sponsors

Ask a number of companies or restaurants to donate items for an inning giveaway during a home game. The company name and location will be announced throughout their inning and a fan will win the donated prize. Figure 1.11 is an example of a letter inviting companies to be inning sponsors.

December

- Verify scrimmage date and times
- Take pictures for the media guide
- Hand out diamond club information

January 25, 2004

Dear Subway,

The softball season is about to begin at Clovis High School and we would like for you to consider making a donation to our program. In the past, different companies have generously donated items that we have used as prizes to award to our fans at home games.

If at all possible, we would like to include your generous company as an inning sponsor. We ask our inning sponsors to donate five items to be given away, but any donation you could make at this time would be very appreciated.

As an inning sponsor, your company's name and location would be announced throughout your inning at each home game.

Thank you so much for your contribution to the Clovis High Softball program. Your efforts help make all of us proud of our involvement in Cougar Softball.

If there is anything we can help you with, please don't hesitate to call.

Thanks again,

Mike Noel
Cougar Softball

Figure 1.11. Inning sponsor letter

- Make hotel reservations for trips
- Schedule umpires
- Plan for team special days

Verifying Scrimmage Date and Times

Although the season has already been scheduled, you should always verify the playing date, time, and location of a scrimmage.

Taking Pictures for the Media Guide

Picture day should obviously be after your season begins, but you'll need to schedule a photographer well in advance. You should invite the local media out to take both posed and action shots. Also, ask your school newspaper to send a photographer to take some action shots for use on your team web site. You might also consider taking a team picture at the end of the season to ensure you have a picture that includes all of the players that finished the season.

Handing Out Diamond Club Information

Consider creating a club for girls in the area to generate interest in the program and to get them acquainted with your coaching style and expectations. Make membership available for $60.00 to girls in grades two through eight. Membership benefits could include:

- Free admission to all home games
- The opportunity to meet and visit with the coaches and players at club functions and games
- Four clinics offered throughout the spring (February, early April, late April, May)
- A media guide, decals, and pencils
- A softball t-shirt

Offer the options of attending the clinics without joining the club ($15.00 per clinic), or joining the club and not attending the clinics ($15.00). Alter these prices to fit your needs. Remember, the primary purpose of the club is to generate interest in the program, so the price of membership is only to cover expenses.

Making Hotel Reservations for Trips

Make reservations for clinics or conventions you might be attending, as well as any out-of-town tournaments in which you'll be playing.

Scheduling Umpires

Send a completed schedule to the secretary of the umpire chapter you have chosen. At least one day before each game, confirm that you have umpires for the game. If it is your responsibility to fill out umpire pay sheets after each game, get them from the athletic director or use the form in Figure 1.12.

ANYWHERE INDEPENDENT SCHOOL DISTRICT
INVOICE FOR FEES
PAID TO SOFTBALL UMPIRES

Date: ____________ Number of Games: _____

___ Varsity ___ Jr. Varsity ___ 9th Grade ___ 8th Grade ___ 7th Grade

OFFICIAL INFORMATION:

Name: ______________________ SS# ______________

Address: ______________________________________

PAY SCALE	
1 game	$17.00
2 games	$35.00
3 games	$60.00

NUMBER OF GAMES WORKED

- ☐ 1 game
- ☐ 2 games
- ☐ 3 games

Total mileage ______ @ $0.32 per mile = $ __________

Fee due for officiating = $ __________

Total due = $ __________

Figure 1.12. Umpire pay sheet

Planning for Team Special Days

Have a meeting and decide specific dates for the team special days. These days include trips to college games, playoff games, sleepovers, scavenger hunts, laser tag, etc. The idea behind these days is to break up the monotony of daily practices, to build team unity, and to give you an opportunity to get out of "coach mode" and have some fun with the girls. Try to schedule one team day per month.

January

- Enlist an announcer
- Get a coaches packet ready
- Meet with all coaches
- Order bathrooms
- Choose a motivational theme
- Prepare themes for the week
- Post goal charts

Enlisting an Announcer

Find someone who is articulate, energetic, has a great "announcing" voice, and is reliable. The announcer should be on the field at least 30 minutes prior to the scheduled game time in order to get all the lineups. Figure 1.13 shows an excellent guideline script for the announcer.

Getting a Coaches Packet Ready

Include the following items in your coaches packets:

- *Agenda for meeting*

    7:30   Introductions of coaches

PUBLIC ADDRESS SCRIPT

1. Be on the field at least 30 minutes prior to the scheduled game time in order to get all the line-ups.

2. **Five minutes before game time**, the coaches will exchange line-up cards and go over the ground rules at home plate. At this time, you will announce the starting line-up.

"Good afternoon, ladies and gentlemen, and welcome to Cougar Park. This afternoon's game features the _____ vs. the Cougars of Clovis High."

"And now for the starting line-ups. First, for the visiting _____ who enter today's game with a record of _____ .

Leading off and playing _____,# _____, _____
Batting 2nd and playing _____,# _____, _____
Batting 3rd and playing _____, # _____, _____
Batting 4th and playing _____, # _____, _____
Batting 5th and playing _____, # _____, _____
Batting 6th and playing _____, # _____, _____
Batting 7th and playing _____, # _____, _____
Batting 8th and playing _____, # _____, _____
Batting 9th and playing _____, # _____, _____
and, _____, # _____, _____

The head coach of the _____ is _____.

And now for the 2004 Clovis High Cougars, who enter today's game with a record of _____.

Leading off and playing _____,# _____, _____
Batting 2nd and playing _____,# _____, _____
Batting 3rd and playing _____, # _____, _____
Batting 4th and playing _____, # _____, _____
Batting 5th and playing _____, # _____, _____
Batting 6th and playing _____, # _____, _____
Batting 7th and playing _____, # _____, _____
Batting 8th and playing _____, # _____, _____
Batting 9th and playing _____, # _____, _____
and, _____, # _____, _____

The head coach of the Cougars is Mike Noel. He is assisted by Tim Douglas and Leland Grigsby."

3. **As the team takes the field:** "The 2004 Clovis Cougars!"

4. **Just as the pitcher reaches the mound:** "Ladies and gentlemen, would you please rise for the playing of our national anthem."

5. **As the pitcher begins her warm-ups:** "The battery for the Cougars, catching number _____, _____ and pitching number _____, _____ ."

6. **After introducing the battery for the home team**, introduce the umpires: "The umpires for today's game are, behind the plate, _____, and on the bases, _____ ."

7. **In the bottom of the first inning,** as their pitcher begins warming up: "The battery for the _____, catching number _____, _____, and pitching number _____, _____ ."

8. **As each batter steps into the batter's box:** "Leading off the (top/bottom) of the _____ inning, number _____, _____." Announce each succeeding hitter by position, number, and name.

9. **At the end of the inning,** announce the runs scored, hits and errors: "For the _____, runs _____, hits _____, and errors _____ ."

10. **At the end of the fifth inning,** announce the next home game and any road game of the week.

11. **At the end of the game,** five the final score and invite fans to the next game.

12. Any other announcements during the course of the game should be done at the discretion of the announcer, including inning sponsor information and give-aways.

    Announcement #1: _____
    Announcement #2: _____
    etc.

Figure 1.13. Public address script (Used with permission from *Baseball/Softball Playbook* by Ron Polk and Donna LoPiano)

7:40   Philosophy of coaching

- ✓ expectations
- ✓ discipline of athletes
- ✓ attitude

8:00   Job descriptions

8:20   Technique and philosophy discussion

10:00 Break

10:10 Technique and philosophy discussion (cont.)

11:30 Staff discussion

- ✓ Missed practices
- ✓ Leadership
- ✓ Motivation
- ✓ Pre-game
- ✓ Grades
- ✓ Attendance
- ✓ Team policies
- ✓ Other

12:00 Dismiss

- *Job descriptions*

The following examples illustrate the assigned duties for a typical staff of four high school coaches (head coach and three assistants) and two junior high coaches.

❑ Coach #1

- ✓ Assist the varsity head coach with practices and in games.
- ✓ Coach first base.
- ✓ Lead field crew during tournament.
- ✓ Call in scores and stats after games.
- ✓ Prepare the end-of-season report for all levels.
- ✓ Post computer printout of individual and team stars after each game.

- ✓ Coordinate academic and tutorial programs.
- ✓ Coordinate winter workout program.
- ✓ Put a player list in teachers' boxes three days prior to out-of-town trips.
- ✓ Compile a needs list for purchasing.
- ✓ Oversee maintenance of field.
- ✓ Manage travel-request and return-travel forms.
- ✓ Develop in-season and off-season weight program.
- ✓ Schedule officials.
- ✓ Keep scouting report during game.
- ✓ Lock up in the evenings and after games.

❑ Coach #2

- ✓ Act as the head junior varsity coach.
- ✓ Give out locker and lock assignments.
- ✓ Maintain all lists (for example, telephone, locker combinations, ID#'s).
- ✓ Coordinate use of equipment.
- ✓ Submit completed inventory sheets and keep up-to-date records on all equipment.
- ✓ Maintain a neat and orderly equipment room.
- ✓ Make sure that players do not wear equipment home.
- ✓ Submit inventory of equipment two weeks after season is over.
- ✓ Manage roll check, board, and record for office.
- ✓ Supervise managers (grades, duties during practices and games, out-of-town checkout).
- ✓ Assist with academics.
- ✓ Supervise locker room.

❑ Coach #3

- ✓ Act as head freshman coach.

- ✓ Coordinate scouting.

- ✓ Coordinate recruitment of young players.

- ✓ Make and print team rosters (include number, name, position, classification).

- ✓ Manage the care and prevention of injuries.

- ✓ Keep file on all athletes (physicals, medical history, emergency numbers, etc.).

- ✓ Submit a needs list of medical items at the end of the season.

- ✓ Manage all strength testing, charts, workout cards, and motivational record boards.

- ✓ Assist with academics.

- ✓ Supervise the locker room.

- ❑ Junior high coaches

  - ✓ Plan the daily practice schedule for junior high athletes.

  - ✓ Monitor academics of junior high athletes.

  - ✓ Maintain attendance list, including ID #'s.

  - ✓ Take care of early dismissals for out-of-town trips; put lists in teachers' boxes three days prior to each trip.

  - ✓ Type team rosters and have them ready to distribute at games.

  - ✓ Provide game-summary report to high school varsity coach by 8:00 am following game day.

  - ✓ Manage roll check board and attendance record; report to high school varsity coach daily.

  - ✓ Oversee equipment issue and inventory records; coordinate needs with high school program.

  - ✓ Organize junior high parent meeting; notify high school varsity coach when it will be held.

  - ✓ Supervise locker room.

- • *Program policies*

- • *Academic plan* (See activities for October in this chapter.)

Meeting with All Coaches

It is very important to meet with all your coaches from all levels prior to every season. You will find it very helpful if the elementary, junior high, and high school coaches are all teaching the same techniques and using similar approaches. The packets you have compiled should cover every aspect of your program. At the meeting, ask coaches for their shirt, shoe, and hat sizes so you have the information for ordering.

Ordering Bathrooms

If your facility does not have on-site bathrooms, you may need to order some.

Choosing a Motivational Theme

Motivation can be an integral part of the success of your team. Choose a theme that can be represented by something tangible and give that tangible item to each athlete. Whatever tangible item you use, decide how it relates to your team as a motivational tool and introduce it at your initial team meeting or at a team retreat. Some examples include:

Paperclip: Make a long chain of 2-3" clips. Explain that each clip represents each athlete's link to the team. Distribute the clips to the players to hang on their purses, backpacks, etc. as a constant reminder that they are a part of the team.

Boomerang: Find inexpensive boomerangs and paint them using school colors. Ask the team, "What does a boomerang do?" Explain that, in life, what you put in to something comes back to you.

Preparing Themes for the Week

In addition to a special theme, spend some time each week emphasizing a certain character trait (courage, loyalty, boldness, decisiveness, dependability, etc.) and decorate the locker room

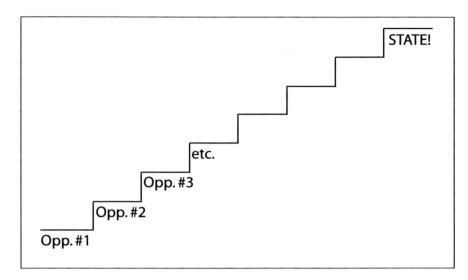

Figure 1.14. Sample goal charts

with quotes that correspond to that trait. The signs can be done on a computer by your managers and can be posted on lockers, doors, and bulletin boards.

Posting Goal Charts

You might post several different goal charts according to your priorities. Figure 1.14 offers two examples.

February

- Have a softball dinner
- Verify transportation
- Contact media
- Arrange national anthem performances
- Make itineraries for trips
- Host a parents meeting
- Meet with civic groups
- Order coaches shirts and hats
- Distribute goodwill gifts to administration and VIPs
- Talk with clubs and organizations
- Have an intrasquad scrimmage
- Mail the media guide
- Issue equipment
- Organize yourself
- Plan a team retreat
- Vote on a unity council
- Choose a manager
- Train a videographer

Having a Softball Dinner

Have a "meet the team" dinner. This event will be a great fundraiser for the program and a way for the community to meet the players. Have a raffle, a silent auction, door prizes, and a table set up to sell booster wear.

Verifying Transportation

Your travel paperwork should be in already. Take time to verify you have transportation and a driver at least three days before each away game.

Contacting Media

Contact all the local or semi-local radio and news stations, as well as the newspapers in your area, and ask if they would cover a few of your games. It doesn't hurt to ask, especially if they cover football games in the area. Provide them all with information about your team. It may spark interest and it might provide them with story ideas. The information can come in many forms: your team web site address, a media guide, or something as easy as a statistic sheet from the past season.

Arranging National Anthem Performances

Ask the band director to tape the band playing the national anthem or enlist individual band members to play. Recruit other talented individuals to either play or sing the anthem as well. Call each individual a few days before each game.

Making Itineraries for Trips

If you are fortunate enough to take an out-of-town trip to a tournament, you'll need to be well-organized. Make out an itinerary and include the hotel address and phone number, van assignments, room assignments, a packing checklist (uniform and equipment), and a tournament schedule. Refer to Figure 1.15.

Hosting a Parents Meeting

Include the date of your meeting in your letters to the athletes. Your parent meeting should address the following subjects:

- Introduction
  - ❑ Background
  - ❑ Success you've had as a coach (or anticipated success)
- Explanation of philosophy

ROAD TRIP ITINERARY

Embassy Suites Hotel
1919 Anywhere Street
Mayberry, TX 77449
(987) 555-1234

TUESDAY, MARCH 13th

3:30 - 4:00	Van check-in (see list)
4:00	VANS LEAVE CLOVIS HIGH (pullovers)
11:00	Arrive in Mayberry/ Check-in hotel
12:00	In rooms for bed check

WEDNESDAY, MARCH 14th

9:00 - 10:00	Breakfast as a team (practice gear, white socks)
10:00 - 11:00	Study table
11:15	Leave for practice
11:30 - 1:00	Practice
1:00 - 3:00	Relax around the hotel (snack stop after practice)
3:00 - 4:00	Study table
4:00 - 6:00	Team activities (long sleeve t-shirt)
6:00 - 7:00	Dinner as a team (location to be announced)
7:00 - 8:00	Motivational talk (speaker to be announced)
8:00 - 10:00	Team activities
10:30	in rooms for bed check

THURSDAY, MARCH 15th

7:00	Breakfast as a team (location to be announced)
8:00 - 10:00	Relax around hotel
10:00	Leave for fields (white uniforms)
12:00	GAME VS. MT. PILOT (1:00)

Times to be announced

FRIDAY, MARCH 16th

Times to be announced (blue uniforms)

SATURDAY, MARCH 17th

8:00	Vans leave for Clovis (long sleeve t-shirt)
5:00	ARRIVE AT CLOVIS HIGH

Van Assignments

Coach Noel	Coach Douglas	Coach Grisgby
H. Reed	Mr. Douglas	Coach Romy
N. Willis	J. Cervantez	M. Barr
J. Reynolds	B. Geary	A. Altamiran
J. Johnson	S. Johnson	C. Shackelford
D. Davila	B. Paillet	A. Castanon
N. Johnson		

Room Assignments

Room 1	Room 2	Room 3	Room 4
Reynolds	Johnson, N.	Shackelford	Johnson, J.
Geary	Cervantez	Reed	Castanon
Davila	Paillet	Johnson, S.	Altamiran
Willis	Barr		

Figure 1.15. Trip itinerary

- Conduct of athletes
  - ✓ Class, character, commitment to excellence
  - ✓ Train hard to become active contributors to society
  - ✓ Alcohol and drug violations; punishment involved
- Academics
  - ✓ Tutoring program
  - ✓ Grade checks
- Keys to success
  - ✓ Mental attitude
  - ✓ Developing winning potential
  - ✓ Athletes will be prepared
- Multi-extracurricular athletes
  - ✓ Athletes will be involved in extracurricular activities
  - ✓ Conflicting schedules will be resolved by coach, teacher, and student

- Discipline
  - Disrespect to teachers and coaches
    - ✓ Conditioning program will be administered
    - ✓ Behavior agreement (see Figure 1.16)
  - Alcohol and drug violations
    - ✓ First offense
    - ✓ Second offense
    - ✓ Third offense
  - Missed practices
    - ✓ Excused
    - ✓ Unexcused
- Closing – question and answer time

Meeting with Civic Groups

Take the time to meet with your local civic groups. Take some of your players with you and be sure to take some schedules, media guides, or anything else that will promote your program. Invite the

---

BEHAVIOR AGREEMENT

Date: _____

Dear _____,

I want to apologize for the way I've been acting in your class. Because of my poor behavior, Coach Jordan has put me in a reminder program until you decide my behavior has improved. Once you feel it has improved, please sign this sheet and return it to Coach Jordan.

Thank you very much,

_____

Instructor: _____ Date: _____
                (signature)

Figure 1.16. Behavior agreement form

groups to your games, preview your goals for the upcoming season, and inform them about any fundraising you might be putting together.

Ordering Coaches Shirts and Hats

When ordering the shirts and hats, be sure to order additional items for administrators and VIPs.

Distributing Goodwill Gifts to Administration and VIPs

The gifts should include media guides, coaches game shirts, and hats, if your program budget will allow.

Talking with Clubs and Organizations

Find out when the clubs and organizations within your school meet and send players to visit with them about attendance at the softball games. If you have a Fellowship of Christian Athletes chapter, for example, set aside an FCA night with free admission for any members and reserved seating as a group. Have the announcer acknowledge the group during breaks.

Having an Intrasquad Scrimmage

During mid-February, have an intrasquad scrimmage. Consider promoting the event and having a family luncheon immediately following the games. Serve pizza and have the players supply side dishes, beverages, desserts, and snacks.

Mailing the Media Guide

The media guide is a great tool for promoting your program. Send it to businesses, newspaper writers, radio stations, etc.

Issuing Equipment

Use a checkout chart to keep track of equipment (see Figure 1.17).

Organizing Yourself

Keep a notebook dedicated to softball only, and divide it into the following sections:

- Schedules – Include your team's schedule and a copy of each conference/district opponent's schedule.

- Student information sheets – Before the season begins, have each athlete fill out an information card with her name, address, phone numbers (cell, home, work), e-mail address, birth date, shoe size, pant size, shirt size, and class schedule. After your manager types it in alphabetically, put your copy in the notebook.

- Roster – Include classification, height, name, and number.

- Eligibility forms – These forms can be acquired from your athletic director's office. Check on the requirements for your state and school.

- Inventory sheet

- Transportation requests – Put a copy of each completed bus request in this section, so you'll have documentation in case of a mix-up.

- Purchase orders – Use your purchase orders to check off equipment as it arrives. These forms can be used to help with inventory as well.

- Inning sponsors – Keep a list of who has donated items for inning giveaways.

- National anthem performers – List the names and phone numbers of the performers and give them a call a couple of days in advance of each game.

- Important phone numbers – List the name and phone number of the person you'll need to call if an umpire doesn't show (usually the head of your umpire chapter). Also, list the names and numbers of the athletic director, the principal, and each coach of each team you will be playing.

- District/conference notes and rules – Once a week, the chairperson of the district usually sends results to each coach with team standings and

2004 Softball Season Equipment Checkout Sheet				
Name	Shirt #	Shorts #	Shoe Sz.	Ret?

Figure 1.17. Equipment checkout sheet

scores. Include any rule changes or other pertinent information about the district or conference.

- Workout notes – Compile a master list of skills and situations for your sport. Keep your workout notes so that every area is covered. These notes can be a valuable tool for the next year as well.

- Drills – As you find drills you like, either from this book, other books, the Internet, journals, or clinics, make copies and put them in your folder for easy reference. You may want to categorize your drills into subsections (e.g. defense, hitting, baserunning, etc.).

- Stat sheets – The day after a match, the managers should enter all statistics into the computer and print a copy for you and a copy to post for the athletes to see.

Planning a Team Retreat

An ideal time to do the retreat would be the day after basketball and soccer season ends. If you cannot afford to dedicate an entire day, then combine some of the following activities to fit your schedule.

- 10:30-10:45 – Welcome and brief introductions

Use a good icebreaker to get things started.

- 10:45-11:30 – Bookshelf activity

These 45 minutes are set aside for reflection on how each individual can put aside anything that could disrupt the team. In the bookshelf activity, explain that we all have a certain amount of "dead weight" that can hinder or hurt us individually or as a team. Say, "As you come into this season, what do you need to leave on the 'bookshelf' as you come into the room?"

- 11:30-12:00 – Refrigerator magnets

Choose an activity that will give everyone more insight on each teammate and coach, for example the refrigerator magnet activity. Explain that refrigerator magnets are fun and descriptive. Ask, "What magnets would I see on your refrigerator if I came over for a visit?"

- 12:00-2:00 – Lunch

Order pizza and have the players bring their own drinks.

- 2:00-4:00 – Team building activities

Use this time to go through a ropes course, or go to a park, split the team into two groups, give them a map and a compass, and select an ending point to meet at. These are just two examples; look at team building books for other ideas. If you don't feel comfortable with this type of team building activity, have a practice.

- 4:00-4:45 – Pass out uniforms

Receiving their team uniforms will help the players get excited about the upcoming season.

- 4:45-5:15 – "What can you bring to the table?"

Ask athletes to reflect on what they can contribute to the team. Make a simple one-page form with questions that will get your players thinking about what they can bring to the team. For example: What specific skills can you bring to the park that will help us be successful?

- 5:15-5:30 – Preparation for dinner

Invite parents and the athletic director to eat a potluck dinner with the team. Assign dishes by position, for example, pitchers and catchers bring pastas, infielders bring salads, and outfielders bring desserts.

- 5:30-6:30 – Dinner and clean-up
- 6:30-7:30 – Introduce theme

Explain your tangible item and how it relates to the theme for the season. If using the boomerang, for example, use this time to have each athlete personalize her boomerang, listing the things she wants to come back to her.

Voting on a Unity Council

As adults and coaches, you are more knowledgeable than your athletes. At the same time, you still need to listen to them. A good way to listen to your players is to have your team vote for members of a unity council that will meet with you on a weekly basis to just talk about "things." This council should be comprised not just with your team captains, but also with a fair number of representatives from the team. Although they may or may not have legitimate gripes, the council is a good way to stay in touch with your team. During the off-season, take this unity council to visit other schools that have successful programs and let your athletes see what other teams are doing to prepare for the next season. Let them see how hard those teams are working, and then your athletes will realize they can work harder or that what they are doing now will pay off later.

Choosing a Manager

The most valuable people you can have on your staff are responsible, trustworthy, and willing student managers. After the season begins and some athletes realize that the sport is not for them, consider asking them to stay with the team and become managers. Give them a job description so they know exactly what is expected of them.

Manager Duties and Expectations

❑ General

- Attend all practices and games.

- Be willing and ready to do any tasks that are asked of you.

- Stay positive and give that impression to the coach.

- Be organized and efficient at the games.

- Act like you know what you're doing and ask for help only when necessary.

- Assist the team and coach whenever you can.

❑ At games

- Fill out the scorebook and stat sheets and have them ready for the game.

- Shag for coaches during warm-up.

- If you have any questions during the game, ask the opposing team's manager first. If that individual can't help and the matter can't wait, ask the coach.

- Make sure the scoring book is correct after the game. If needed, compare with the other team's book after the game.

- Videotape the games.

❑ At practices

- Shag for coaches.

- Summarize stats and put into the computer.

- Take stats as needed.

- Set up field and hitting area for daily drills prior to practice.

- Clean up and organize field and hitting area following practice.

- Ask the coach if any specific jobs need to be done.

- Make inspiring signs for the locker room.

- If really bored, replace material on bulletin boards.

- Help team and coaches as needed.

Training a Videographer

One of the managers can be designated as videographer as long as she knows exactly how you'd like the game filmed. Some tips to ensure a good videotape include:

- Video cameras normally rewind a small amount each time the camera is turned off or even paused. Let at least three to five seconds run off the tape before you stop to prevent erasing good footage. It also takes a few seconds for recording to begin again. Be liberal with the tape as you start and stop filming.

- Try to film from behind centerfield or behind home plate so you're out of everyone's way, or consider filming from an angle behind the on-deck circles if possible. This location will enable you to see whether the hitting mechanics are correct.

- From behind centerfield, start each pitch with a view of the pitcher and hitting area. As the ball is put in play, zoom out to get all the action of the play.

- From behind home plate or from the angle, zoom in on your hitter or your pitcher.

- Keep the camera on a tripod to avoid shaking the camera. Don't talk while filming.

- During time-outs, film the players, coaches, fans, and scoreboard. This footage can be used for the end-of-year video.

- Label the tape with the opponent's name, the date, and the final score.

March

- Take a trip to a college game

- Recognize honor roll students

- Send thank you notes to parents

Taking a Trip to a College Game

Talk with the college coach in advance and ask if your players could spend a little time after the game meeting the college players. This meeting will help motivate your athletes and promotes the college program as well.

Recognizing Honor Roll Students

At each grading period, encourage the principal or athletic director to recognize the athletes that have done well in their academics. Promoting this idea may also encourage other athletes to do better in class.

Sending Thank You Notes to Parents

Take some time to handwrite personal notes to the parents of your players. Having a daughter on the team requires some sacrifices from parents and thanking them for their support is important.

April

- Order senior plaques
- Scout potential playoff opponents
- Prepare for the playoffs
- Arrange a team special day

Ordering Senior Plaques

During the last home game, have "Senior Night." Present each senior with a plaque and flowers. Their teammates might also choose to give them additional gifts. Figure 1.18 gives an example of a script to give the announcer.

Scouting Potential Playoff Opponents

Chapter 7 provides detailed information on how to scout your opponents. Arrange your schedule so you and some of your coaches can attend games of possible playoff opponents.

Preparing for the Playoffs

In addition to the obvious practice planning and preparation to play, you should also consider doing the following:

- Advertise the dates, times, and locations of your games at the school and in the community.
- If you are playing at home, provide extra seating at the field and schedule your announcer and national anthem performances.

Senior Script

#25 Avery Noel

"Avery is a four-year varsity starter who has provided a great deal to her teammates on and off the field. On the field, Avery will finish her career at Clovis High ranked in the career top five in games played, at-bats, runs scored, hits, double, triples, and RBI's. Her ability on the field has lead to many accolades including three All-TRAC selections, two All-Valley picks, two All-West Region selections, and two NFCA All-American honors.

Off the field, Avery has been just as prolific. She has been named Academic All-American by NFCA four times and will graduate in June with a GPA of 3.98.

Avery will be remembered for her caring nature and hard working attitude. Thank you, Avery, for everything you have given us.

Avery is joined on the field by _____.

Avery, we thank you and we love you.

Ladies and Gentlemen, Avery Noel."

Figure 1.18. Senior Night script

- If asked, rank the top five officials you'd like to call the games.

- Submit additional travel requests.

- Double-check grades to avoid playing an ineligible player.

- Have the players prepare in advance for missing any classes by meeting with their teachers and getting assignments.

Arranging a Team Special Day

You may choose to do something non-softball-related at this point. Although you, as a coach, live and breathe the sport, the players might appreciate a diversion. But, you may also consider attending playoff games together as a team if your season is coming to an end.

Photo: David Menedian

Planning the Season

Player Assessment

Have a tryout at the beginning of the season to assess the skills of your players. Although you may have an idea who will make the team, ranking your players will give everyone a fair chance. Some of the following skills tests might be employed to evaluate performance:

- Throwing
  - ❑ Arm strength
  - ❑ Accuracy
- Fielding
  - ❑ Ground balls
  - ❑ Fly balls
- Hitting
  - ❑ Swing
  - ❑ Power
  - ❑ Game at bats
  - ❑ Bunting

- Running
  - ❑ Home to first base
  - ❑ Home to second base
  - ❑ Shuttle run
  - ❑ Game instincts
- Miscellaneous
  - ❑ Accountability
  - ❑ Hustle/enthusiasm
  - ❑ Softball instincts
  - ❑ Specific skill
  - ❑ Sportsmanship

A Formula for Evaluation

Once you have determined the skills you would like to evaluate, put the numbers in the "formula" to rank your players. Use the same scale as track meets, or assign points however you'd like.

Whether or not you post the results of your evaluation for the players to see is up to you. It may be a good motivational technique to use throughout the year or you may choose to use this information for personal use in determining how to organize your teams. It also may become useful if a parent absolutely believes his child should be a starter on varsity. The following example illustrates how you can undertake the evaluative process.

Timed Events

- Step #1: Take 10% of the best time. This percentage enables you to add a fair amount of time regardless of the length of time of each event. As the time for different events gets longer, the range gets longer.

- Step #2: Add the result from step #1 to the best time to get a range.

    Example: Home to first base

    Best time = 3.3

    Take 3.3 x 0.10 = 0.33 (round to nearest tenth)

    Add 0.3 to best time (3.3 + 0.3 = 3.6) to get range for 10 points. The chart illustrated in Figure 2.1 can be used for the entire scale.

Timed Event Chart

3.3 - 3.6 = 10 points
3.7 - 4.0 = 8 points
4.1 - 4.4 = 6 points
4.5 - 4.8 = 4 points
4.9 - 5.2 = 2 points
5.3 - 5.6 = 1 point

Figure 2.1. Timed event chart

Skill Events

- Step #1: Take the best attempt and assign it 10 points. (Or assign points according to number of attempts, i.e. 11 made catches = 11 points.)

- Step #2: The next-best attempt gets eight points, etc. The chart in Figure 2.2 can be used to assign points for skill events.

Skill Event Chart

12 catches = 10 points
11 catches = 8 points
10 catches = 6 points
9 catches = 4 points
8 catches = 2 points
7 catches = 1 point

Figure 2.2. Skill event chart

Explanation of Events

Throwing

❑ Arm strength

This skill is graded subjectively. To test the players, pair them up and have them play catch at a long distance. This test can be done during their warm-up.

❑ Accuracy

To test the players' throwing accuracy, line up the girls at 60 feet and 120 feet away from a protective net. Give each girl five throws from both distances and count how many times she hits the net. The girls are rated on a 10-point system. If a player hits the net six times, she's rated a six.

Fielding

❑ Ground balls and fly balls

To test the players' ability as fielders, give each girl 10 ground balls of varying types (right at her, to the right, to the left, slow rollers, high hoppers, etc.) and grade her ability to make the play. For the outfielders, incorporate some fly balls into their 10 chances.

Hitting

❏ Swing

During the allowed time for hitting, give each player 10 swings off of a machine. You could either score each result a one (ball put in play) or a zero (ball not put in play) to give a score of 0 through 10. Another way to score this test is to give a subjective score, rating the actual mechanics of the swing.

❏ Power

Because many of the girls trying out won't show many signs of power throughout the week, give this trait a subjective score based on body type and swing mechanics.

❏ Game at bats

During the two days of games, give each player 10 game at bats. Grade each at bat on how effective it was. For example, if the player reaches base, moves a runner over, or makes great contact, give those at bats a one. If she doesn't have a productive at bat, give that a zero. If a player has seven productive at bats, she is given a rating of seven. You can also give bonus points for extra-base hits, RBIs, etc.

❏ Bunting

To test the players on their bunting ability, have each girl bunt 10 pitches from a pitching machine, either at home plate or in an open area around the ballpark, such as the outfield or a hitting tunnel. Each bunt she successfully gets down earns her a point. If a player has success on four bunts, she is rated a four.

Running

❏ Home to first base

Have the players line up at home plate, where a batting tee is placed. One at a time, the players, from the batter's box, hit a ball off the tee and run to first base. Start the clock as the bat makes contact with the ball and stop it as the player makes contact with first base.

❏ Home to second base

Have the players line up at home plate, where a batting tee is placed. One at a time, the players, from the batter's box, hit a ball off the tee and run to second base. Start the clock as the bat makes contact with the ball and stop it as the player makes contact with second base.

❏ Shuttle run

Set up three cones 10 feet apart. Each player starts by straddling the middle cone. On the command, she shuffles to the right cone, then shuffles to the far left cone, and finishes by running through the middle cone. Refer to Figure 2.3.

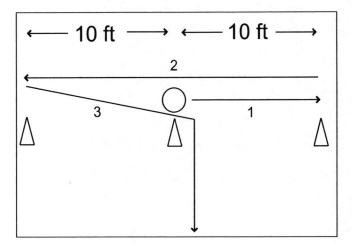

Figure 2.3. Shuttle run

❏ Instincts

A player's instincts on the bases is a subjective score. As you observe the games, make notes of how each player reacts on the bases. Do they know what to do? Are they aggressive? If you do not see enough base running from each player, set up a drill that will put the players in decision-making situations.

Split the girls up into three groups (at first base, second base, and third base). Put a ball in play from home plate and see how each base reacts. For example, if the ball is hit on the ground to the shortstop's right, the runner from third should read it and go. The runner at second should read it to see if it goes through or is fielded. The runner at first goes immediately.

Miscellaneous

❑ Accountability

This test is a subjective score. You can base it on attendance at the tryouts and any meetings, whether players are tardy, if they turn in all paperwork on time, and their performance in the classroom. This category can be used for anything you feel the players are responsible for taking care of.

❑ Hustle/Enthusiasm

This category is subjective. Rate players on their overall hustle and energy level throughout the tryout.

❑ Softball instincts

This item is a subjective score. Watch the games carefully and check the players' instincts. Do they back up bases? Do they recognize a bunt situation? These instincts can all be taught, but looking for them could help you identify who's mentally ready for what level.

❑ Specific skill

This area is where you can reward a player if she brings to the field one or more special factors. For example, if a player is very inexperienced as a softball player, but can really run fast, you might have a need for her as a pinch runner. Another example is someone who can pitch. Pitching is a special skill that can really help out your program and needs to be given extra consideration.

❑ Sportsmanship

This area is also subjective. Check to see who exhibits good teammate qualities. Picking up gear, a pat on the back of a dejected teammate, and positive comments all say a lot about what kind of chemistry each girl will bring to your team.

Sample Evaluation Form

You'll need a form to record times, attempts, and comments for your entire team. Use the form in Figure 2.4 as an example. Each athlete should have her own evaluation form as well (Figure 2.5). It may seem like a lot of paperwork, but utilize your assistant coaches or managers to transfer information.

Tryout Schedule

Carefully plan your schedule so no time is wasted. Utilize your assistants and managers, and stay on time.

Tuesday

2:50 – 3:10	Sign-up/Introduction
3:10 – 3:20	Stretch
3:20 – 3:30	Warm up arms
3:30 – 3:50	Ground balls/Fly balls
3:50 – 4:30	Bunting/Fielding with throws
4:30 – 4:45	Running from home to first three times
3:50 – 4:45	Returnees – Hitting area

Name	throw/a	throw/s	field	hit	bunt	H>1	H>2	Shuttle	Game	GPA
Allen, T. 11	4	4	4	1	4	3.87	7.97	7.01	3-9 3 ks	1.71
Burke, S 11	6	6	8	6	3	3.51	7.10	5.47	2-9	3.60
Davis, Z.10	6	6	6	5	4	4.51	8.68	7.00	7-9	3.33

Figure 2.4. Team evaluation form

```
┌─────────────────────────────────────────────────────────────┐
│                   Individual Evaluation Report                │
│                                                               │
│   Name: _____        Grade: _____      │
│                                                               │
│   1.  Throwing      Arm Strength      _____                  │
│                     Accuracy          _____                  │
│                                                               │
│   2.  Fielding      GB/FB             _____                  │
│                     Versatility       _____                  │
│                                                               │
│   3.  Hitting       Swing             _____                  │
│                     Power             _____                  │
│                     Game              _____                  │
│                     Bunting           _____                  │
│                                                               │
│   4.  Running       Home to first     _____                  │
│                     Home to second    _____                  │
│                     Shuttle           _____                  │
│                     Instincts         _____                  │
│                                                               │
│   5.  Misc.         Accountability    _____                  │
│                     Hustle/Enthusiasm _____                  │
│                     SB Instincts      _____                  │
│                     Specific Skill    _____                  │
│                     Sportsmanship     _____                  │
│                                                               │
│   6.  Comments:                                               │
│                                                               │
└─────────────────────────────────────────────────────────────┘
```

Figure 2.5. Individual evaluation report

Wednesday

3:00 – 3:05	Stretch
3:05 – 3:10	Warm up arms
3:10 – 3:40	Throwing accuracy
3:40 – 4:30	Hitting off of machine (10 swings)
4:30 – 4:45	Running from home to second two times
3:40 – 4:45	Returnees – Hitting area

Thursday

3:00 – 3:10	Stretch
3:10 – 3:20	Warm up arms
3:20 – 3:30	Ground balls/Fly balls
3:30 – 4:30	Game
4:30 – 4:45	Shuttle run two times
3:30 – 4:45	Returnees – Hitting area

Friday

3:00 – 3:10	Stretch
3:10 – 3:20	Warm up arms
3:20 – 4:30	Game
3:20 – 4:45	Returnees – Hitting area

Choosing the Teams

As coaches, you know life is full of challenges and disappointments, but that's hard for most young women to understand. If you have to cut players, then bring each one in and talk to her personally rather than posting a list. Show them their evaluation forms and talk to them about how they can improve in the off-season. Help them accept this decision and offer alternatives if possible.

Assigning Players to Positions

Pitcher

Characteristics:
- strong presence on and off the field
- positive and competitive way about her

Abilities:
- three quality pitches, including a change-up
- good athlete, able to field her position

Catcher

Characteristics:
- take-charge demeanor
- coach on the field

Abilities:
- knowledge of the game
- strong and quick athlete
- strong arm
- quick release

First Base

Characteristics:
- left-handed thrower is a plus
- aggressive attitude on bunts

Abilities:
- moves forward quickly
- quick reactions

Second Base

Characteristics:
- best athlete
- quick feet

Ability:
- moves quickly from side to side

Shortstop

Characteristics:
- good athlete
- able to direct traffic in the infield

Abilities:
- strong arm
- moves quickly from side to side

Third Base

Characteristic:
- aggressive attitude on bunts

Abilities:
- moves forward quickly
- quick reactions

Left Field

Characteristic:
- aggressive

Abilities:
- weakest arm of the three outfielders
- good at moving side to side

Center Field

Characteristics:
- aggressive
- take-charge attitude
- leader of the outfield

Abilities:
- good at coming in and going back on balls
- strong arm

Right Field

Characteristic:
- aggressive

Abilities:

- strongest arm of the three outfielders
- good at moving side to side

Pinch Runner

Characteristics:

- aggressive
- ready to go when called upon

Abilities:

- running speed
- base running instincts

Individual Roles

Each player should have clearly defined individual field roles. Use the following examples as a guide.

2003 Cougar Softball

Jennifer Reynolds: the "rock" that the team can count on, game control from the circle, consistency on offense, a run producer.

Jenna Cervantez: provide a spark on offense from the top of the order, smart and aggressive on the base paths, provide leadership for the infield.

Merryann Barr: run producer from the middle of the order, solid in the circle, aggressive play from first base, push teammates.

Alexia Castanon: solid defensive contributor, aggressiveness from the hot corner, consistent RBI producer.

Desiree Davila: versatility throughout the lineup, scrappy play in the field, on the bases, and at the plate, high on-base percentage.

Jessica Johnson: leader of the outfield, exceptional bat control from the two hole, ability to reach base, aggressiveness.

Heather Reed: provide stability in the lineup, run producer, provide leadership on and off the field.

Britney Paillet: exceptional defense, consistently put pressure on the defense, supportive.

Nicole Settlemyer: run the game from behind the plate, provide energy, help increase the focus level of the entire team.

Natalie Johnson: provide support and energy for teammates, provide aggressive base running.

Courtney Shackelford: provide energy, go-to player off the bench.

Choosing Your Game Plan

The game plan you choose should be based on the level, skill, and experience of your team. With an experienced, talented varsity team, you might decide to be very aggressive, using an effective running game, well-executed bunts, the steal, hit-and-run, and an occasional squeeze play. On the other hand, if your players are just beginning to understand the concept of an inning and that each team has nine players on the field at a time, you cannot expect them to be able to perfect every aspect of the game. As a result, you must decide what your team is capable of and focus on those things.

Checklists of Skills

Team Skills

To be successful, you need a master schedule so that all aspects of the game are covered. The following basic checklist (broken down by skill level) is just something to get you started. You have to decide what is important for your team to accomplish before the first game and throughout the season.

Beginner

The most popular group in this category will be your junior high teams, although some freshman or junior varsity teams may fall into this category as well. Make sure these players learn the following:

- Basic fundamentals (throwing, catching, hitting, base running, and fielding)
- Infield and outfield jurisdiction
- Covering bases
- Bunt defense
- Signals
- Sliding
- Cutoffs and relays

Intermediate

Once a team has mastered the beginning level concepts of the game, the following aspects can be addressed:

- Pickoffs
- Double plays
- Hit-and-run
- Bunt-and-run
- First-and-third double steals (offense)
- Bunt offense
- Rundowns

Advanced

The following areas, from a teaching standpoint, are most appropriate for your varsity level athletes who are proficient in their fundamentals and understand the beginning and intermediate concepts of the game fairly well.

- Squeeze play
- Suicide squeeze play
- Safety squeeze play
- Delay steal
- Double steal

Position Skills

Each position also has specific skills that are unique to that position. Some skills can be drilled specifically and others just need mentioning. For example, in the first baseman's checklist, "fielding bunts" should be drilled specifically (see Chapter 3 for drills) and "making sure the runner touches the base" just needs mentioning.

First Base

- Cutoff responsibilities
- Fielding bunts
- 3-6-3 double plays
- Footwork around the bag
- Fielding bad hops
- Tagging first base on the double play attempt
- Fielding ground balls
- Protecting the line
- Flipping the ball to second baseman on ground ball
- Making sure the runner touches the base
- Pickoff play: pitchout, throw to first
- Playing the fence on the pop-up
- Responsibilities on pop-ups in the infield
- Following runner to second base
- Movement by the count
- Backup responsibilities
- Responsibilities on run-downs

Second Base

- Fielding short hops
- Preventing the delayed steal
- Backing up pitcher on throws from catcher
- Covering second base on steal attempt
- Slap tags
- Movement by the count
- Footwork around the bag
- Picking up catcher's signal
- Double steal responsibilities

- Double play situations
  - ☐ 4-6-3
  - ☐ 6-4-3
  - ☐ 5-4-3
  - ☐ 3-6-4
- Cutoff responsibilities
- Relay responsibilities
- Making sure runner touches second base
- Making tag plays from infield and outfield sides
- Responsibilities on bunts
  - ☐ runner at first
  - ☐ runner at second
  - ☐ runner at third
  - ☐ no one on
- Decoying runners
- Rundown responsibilities
- Fielding ground balls
- Pickoff play: pitchout, cover first for throw

Shortstop

- Fielding short hops
- Preventing the delayed steal
- Backing up the pitcher on throws from catcher
- Covering second on steal attempts
- Movement by the count
- Picking up the catcher's signal
- Pickoff plays: third baseman charges, cover third for throw
- Double steal responsibilities
- Double play situations
  - ☐ 4-6-3
  - ☐ 6-4-3
  - ☐ 3-6-3
- Cutoff responsibilities
- Relay responsibilities

- Snap tags
- Making tag plays from infield and outfield sides
- Responsibilities on bunts
  - ☐ runner at first
  - ☐ runner at second
  - ☐ runner at third
- Decoying runners
- Rundown responsibilities
- Fielding ground balls

Third Base

- Fielding ground balls
- Movement by the count
- Movement by the batter
- Responsibilities for fielding pop-ups
- Playing the fence
- Double plays
  - ☐ 5-4-3
  - ☐ 5U-3
- Pickoff plays: throw to third
- Fielding bunts
- Responsibilities on bunts
  - ☐ runner at first
  - ☐ runner at second
  - ☐ runner at third
- Cutoff responsibilities
- Tag plays from infield and outfield sides
- Slap tags
- Decoying the runners
- Backing up pitcher on throws from the first baseman
- Playing the line
- Double steal responsibilities
- Rundown responsibilities

Pitcher

- Fielding bunts
- Fielding bad hops
- Backup responsibilities
- 1-6-3 double plays
- Flipping the ball to first
- Flipping the ball to third
- Pitchouts
- Intentional walks
- Responsibility on rundowns
- Plays at the plate (wild pitch, passed ball)
- Communication with the catcher
- Communication with the infield

Catcher

- Giving signs
  - ❑ no one on base
  - ❑ runner on second base
  - ❑ pitchout
  - ❑ hiding signs
- Proper shifting
- Handling pop-ups
- Tag play at the plate
- Force play at the plate
- Fielding bunts
- Backing up first base
- Handling pitches
- Working with umpires
- Double steal responsibilities
  - ❑ arm fake, throw to third
  - ❑ throw high to pitcher
  - ❑ throw to middle infielder
  - ❑ throw through to second base

- Pickoff plays
  - ❑ pitchout, throw to first
  - ❑ throw to third
- Decoying runners at the plate
- Throwing to bases on steal attempts
- Using cutoff people
- Communication with coaches during game
- Responsibilities on rundown plays
- Calling pitches
- Bringing pitch into the strike zone
- Taking advantage of batter's weakness

Outfield

- Charging ground balls
- Proper fielding technique
- Proper fly ball technique
- Fielding fly balls in the sun
- Movement by situation
- Playing the wind
- Hitting cutoff people
- Throwing to bases
- Picking up stopped ball
- Throwing behind the runner
- Playing the fence
- Backing up bases
- Responsibilities on rundown plays
- Responsibilities on bunt situations
- Responsibilities on pickoff plays
- Communication with other outfielders
- Communication with infielders
- Priorities in the outfield
- Knowing what the situation dictates

Putting It All on a Timeline

Break your season down into phases and determine what your teaching emphasis should be during each phase. Then, write down general areas you want to cover during the week so nothing is left out. Once the season begins, you should refer to this master plan and use it to write detailed practice plans. You will have to make changes according to the development of your team, but having a solid master plan to work from will be helpful.

Phase One (Pre-Season)

*   Cover your checklist of skills.
*   Develop a good conditioning base.

*   Improve individual skills.
*   Implement your offensive and defensive objectives.

Phase Two (In-Season)

*   Note team weaknesses and plan practices to target them.
*   Incorporate pre-game routine.
*   Practice game situation drills daily.

Phase Three (Off-Season)

Follow the detailed plan of action outlined in Chapter 10.

Photo: Leslie Scott

3

Planning a Practice

The time you spend practicing with your team is valuable. Don't waste any of it. If you let your players drag out to the field, then you may have lost three minutes that day. Those three minutes a day over the course of a school year become nine hours of missed practice time. After planning for your season, you have the task of breaking all the planned drills and practices down into individual workouts designed to target the needs of your team. Ensuring that your team's practice is well-organized and well-spent requires that you address several areas, including a general practice outline, a master practice outline, a daily practice schedule, and other practice concerns.

General Practice Outline

Each practice should contain all or part of the following components:

- Meetings (optional)
- Warm-up
- Individual skill work
- Team drills
- Batting practice
- Conditioning
- Bad weather alternatives

Meetings

- Use the time set aside for meetings to:
- Address issues brought up in the leadership council meeting.
- Watch and critique film.
- Discuss a rule of the day.
- Recognize a player for an outstanding or uplifting performance (in the classroom, with the community, etc.).
- Emphasize a character trait (courage, loyalty, boldness, decisiveness, dependability, etc.). A very helpful resource for emphasizing character is the book *Coaching to Change Lives* by The Zig Ziglar Corporation.

Warm-Up

Depending on your philosophy, your team's warm-up should consist of drills and exercises that will prepare your players for a challenging practice.

Long-Distance Jog

Start with a jog of three or four laps around your entire field. This exercise can set the tone for the entire practice. Not only will the run warm up the players' muscles, but the length of the run will immediately bring your players' attention to the practice.

Stretching and Agilities

Spend time stretching all the muscle groups used in softball, including the arms, shoulders, and back. Agilities are not only a great way to ready the muscles and joints for practice, but can also improve your players' running form and quickness. Any track coach should be able to provide you with a wide range of drills to promote proper running form and increase quickness.

Throwing Program

Your throwing program should address four areas: warming up the shoulder, improving throwing technique, increasing arm strength, and improving throwing accuracy. A sample program would look like the following: (The team should be divided into two lines for each drill and your throwing mechanics philosophy should be used.)

- One-knee throws

Have players start 10 feet apart, facing a partner. Each player places the knee of her throwing-arm side on the ground and points her glove-side foot towards her partner (Figure 3.1). The short distance will put an emphasis on technique, not strength. Spend two minutes working on these throws.

- Isolated feet

Players should move 45 feet from each other. Each player points her glove-side foot towards her partner and sets the foot of her throwing-arm side perpendicular to the front foot (Figure 3.2). While keeping the feet planted, except for the allowance of

Figure 3.1. One-knee throws

Figure 3.2. Isolated feet

the back foot to rotate on follow-through, players continue the warm-up. Spend three to five minutes on this drill.

- Long catch

Players should move to a distance of 100 to 150 feet between each other. Have each player throw the ball to her partner, while getting as much height and length on the throw as possible. Long catch is the best way to increase a player's arm strength. Spend three to five minutes on this drill.

- 21 (target catch)

Move players back to a distance of 45 feet between each other. To finish the warm-up, have players concentrate on their accuracy. Using parts of the body as targets, the players should try to accumulate points that total 21 faster than their partner. A throw that is caught in front of the face is 5 points, in front of the chest is 3 points, and the stomach is 1 point. Players must hit 21 exactly or their score drops back to 13.

Not only will the throwing program prepare your team for practice, but it will also get them into the proper mindset. Warming up will become more than just playing catch and talking about your day.

Individual Skill Work

During individual skill work, you should have all players involved in a drill. An efficient way to include all your players in individual skill work is with circuits. Pick and choose from the following drills and develop your own stations. The list of drills is by no means a comprehensive list. It includes a few drills to improve each skill, along with a few of the authors' favorites.

Hitting

❑   Soft Toss

Set-Up: One hitter, one tosser with a bucket of balls, and a screen to hit into.

Directions: The player positions herself about five feet away from the screen while the coach or another player is in front and off to the side of the hitter. The coach or player tosses a ball underhanded to the hitter and the hitter hits the ball into the screen (Figure 3.3).

Figure 3.3. Soft toss

❑ Tee Drill

Set-Up: One hitter, a batting tee, a bucket of balls.

Directions: Have the hitter position the tee on the inside part of the plate. The hitter should hit the ball from the tee, focusing on good hitting technique (Figure 3.4).

Variations:

• The hitter can move the tee to the outside or middle of the plate and adjust the height of the tee to simulate a high or low pitch.

• Add another tee behind the first tee to emphasize swinging down on the ball (Figure 3.5).

❑ Bunting Drill

Set-Up: One hitter, one tosser, and a bucket of balls.

Directions: Position the hitter in front of the tosser and emphasize a good bunting position. The tosser, on one knee, throws the hitter a designated number of balls while the hitter works on different types of bunts (slap, drag, etc.).

Variation: Have the hitter bunt to targets on the ground to improve accuracy.

❑ Hitting Circuit – two players at each station (Figure 3.6)

Station 1 – Live hitting

Station 2 – Shag

Station 3 – Shag

Station 4 – One-armed soft toss

Station 5 – Tee drills

Station 6 – Bunting

Station 7 – Strength

Station 8 – Tunnel with pitching machine

Baserunning

❑ Take-two Drill

Set-Up: One hitter at home plate, other players in a line behind Player 1, coach positioned in the outfield, and one cutoff person in the infield.

Directions: After simulating swing, Player 1 runs towards first base, takes a turn, and reads the throw from the coach in the outfield. If it is a high throw (over the cutoff person's head), she should continue to second. If the throw is cut, she should read the outcome: if cut, stay at first base. If it goes through, she should continue to second.

❑ Stopwatch Drill

Set-Up: One hitter at home plate, one tee, coach with stopwatch, and rest of the team in line behind Player 1.

Figure 3.4. Tee drill

Figure 3.5. Two-tee drill

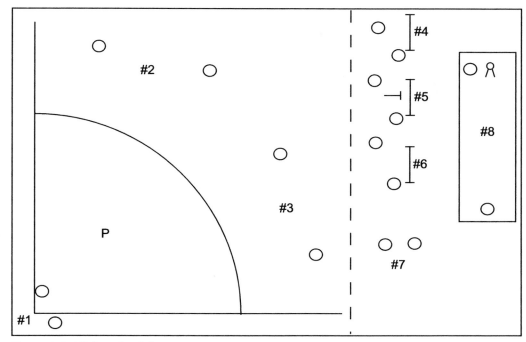

Figure 3.6. Hitting circuit layout

Directions: Have the hitter hit a ball from the tee and sprint to first base. The time starts when the ball is contacted and ends when the hitter touches first base.

Variations: Have hitters run from home to second, second to home on a base hit, or work on steals.

❑ Ball in the Dirt

Set-Up: Three lines of runners down first base line, pitcher in circle, catcher behind home plate.

Directions: Player 1 in each line takes a good lead from the base. Each player reads the trajectory of the ball thrown from the pitcher and gets a good jump. If the ball is in the dirt, the runners should go to second.

❑ Signs Drill

Set-Up: During batting practice, have runners on base.

Directions: While hitters are taking their swings, have base runners take signs from the coach.

For defensive skill work, divide the players into three groups: infielders, outfielders, and catchers. Each coach works with a group on specific drills to improve their individual abilities.

Catchers

❑ Framing Drill

Set-Up: Catchers behind a plate, coach pitching balls.

Directions: Each catcher should receive 10 pitches inside and out, up and down.

Variation: Catchers can also work on framing the ball during work in the bullpen.

❑ Passed Ball Drill

Set-Up: Catcher is behind home plate, coach standing about 10 feet in front of home plate.

Directions: The coach tosses the ball behind the catcher and, while the catcher retrieves the ball, the coach moves up to home plate and receives a throw from the catcher.

❑ Blocking Drill

Set-up: Catcher is at plate in full gear with paddle instead of glove. Coach is 10 to 15 feet away. Use softer balls such as foam balls or tennis balls to decrease injury for an inexperienced catcher or if it is late in the season.

Description: Catcher is in normal catching position. Draw an arc with a three-foot radius in front of the plate. Coach throws ball in the dirt, requiring the catcher to block the ball, keeping it down in front of her within that arc. After five balls in the arc, the catcher exits the drill.

Variations:

• Add an actual softball.

• Increase reps to use this drill as a conditioning drill.

• Transition from the paddle to a glove for a more game-like situation.

• Increase intensity and competition by hitting balls using a fungo bat.

❑ Pop-up Drill

Set-Up: Catcher in full gear at home plate. Coach has bucket of balls and fungo bat.

Description: Catcher starts in normal stance. Coach hits a pop-up. Catcher works on removing mask, making sure it's out of the way, tracking the ball, and catching the ball with her back to the playing field. Players rotate into the drill.

❑ Bunt Drill

Set-Up: Catcher is in full gear at home plate in normal stance. Coach is in the batter's box. Have a player, manager, or coach at first base.

Description: Coach rolls ball in any direction in a 10-foot radius of home plate. Catcher fields the ball and throws to first base. Emphasize to the catcher staying low to the ball, clearing herself from the runner, and making the throw.

Variations:

• Have catchers throw to second and third base.

• Add a runner or barrier to force the catcher to clear.

❑ Steal Defense Drill

Set-Up: Catcher at home plate in full gear. Pitcher or coach in the circle pitching. Player or manager at second base.

Directions: Pitcher pitches the ball to the catcher. Catcher throws to second base.

Variations:

• Use a stopwatch to time from when the ball hits the catcher's glove to when it hits the glove at second base. A good time is around 2.0 seconds.

• Throw to third base.

• Work on the pitchout and throw to second base.

• Add runners.

Infielders

❑ Star Drill

Set-Up: All infielders are in their defensive positions with the first baseman and third baseman covering their bases. The catcher has the ball.

Directions: The catcher begins by throwing to the shortstop. The shortstop throws to the first baseman, the first baseman throws to the third baseman, the third baseman throws to the second baseman, and the second baseman throws back to the catcher. (C-SS-1B-3B-2B-C)

Variation: The catcher starts the drill by throwing to the second baseman. (C-2B-3B-1B-SS-C)

❑ Short Hop Drill

Set-Up: Players in groups of two, 25 to 30 feet apart.

Directions: Player 1 throws ball in dirt. Player 2 fields the short hop and applies a tag.

Variation: Instead of applying a tag, first basemen work on the stretch.

❏ Throwing Drill

Set-Up: Players in groups of two, 10 to 15 feet apart.

Directions: Players work on four types of throws: underhand flip, backhand toss, dart throw, and glove toss. Work each throw for one minute.

❏ Pop-up Drills

Set-Up: Players in a line in front of coach, 20 feet apart.

Directions: Coach tosses a ball over the player's head. Players work on getting back to the ball using crossover or drop steps, keeping arms pumping, and reaching at the last minute to catch the ball.

Variations:

• Work off live bat from home plate.

• Hit right, left, and directly behind players to give them different looks.

❏ Fielding Drill #1

Set-Up: Two hitters with one at the right side of home plate and the other on the left side. Both hitters have shaggers and a bucket of balls. Put empty buckets at first and third base.

Directions: The shortstop receives a ball from the hitter and then fields the ball and throws it to first base. The second baseman receives a ball from the second hitter and then fields the ball and throws to third base. When the hitters' buckets are empty, rotate players and start the drill again.

Variations:

• H1-SS-3B and H2-2B-1B

• H1-SS-3B and H2-1B-2B

• H1-3B-SS (covering 3B) and H2-2B-1B

• H1-2B-3B and H2-1B-SS (covering 2B)

• H1-2B-SS (covering 2B) and H2-1B-3B

• Work on double plays by adding an additional first baseman to receive throws.

• Add the pitcher to work on preventing steals and covering bunts.

Outfielders

❏ Fielding Drill #2

Set-Up: Have a player covering each base, a line of outfielders in each position (LF, CF, RF), and a coach positioned in the infield (refer to Figure 3.7).

Directions: The first person in each of the outfield lines fields a ground ball that is hit or thrown by the coach, then throws it quickly to the appropriate infielder.

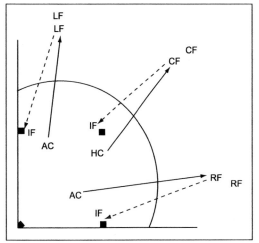

Figure 3.7. Fielding drill #2

❏ Fence Drill

Set-Up: Have two lines of players positioned 10 to 12 feet from the outfield fence. The coach, with a shagger, is stationed in between the lines, facing the fence as illustrated in Figure 3.8.

Directions: The coach tosses a ball against the fence. The two players run to the ball, communicating with one another. As one player calls "ball" and retrieves it, the other outfielder reads the shagger's position and tells the outfielder with the ball where to throw. If the shagger is to the right of the coach, four or home is the call. If the shagger is to the left, the call is three.

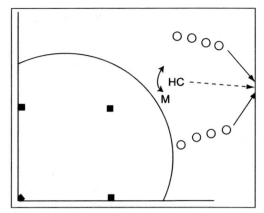

Figure 3.8. Fence drill

❑ Diving Drill

Set-Up: Have two lines of players in the outfield, a coach to toss balls, and a bucket.

Directions: The coach tosses a ball in front of the outfielder. The outfielder performs a bent-leg slide and then returns the ball to the bucket stationed beside the coach (Figure 3.9.)

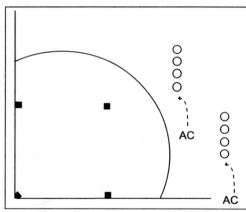

Figure 3.9. Diving drill

❑ Target Throwing Drill

Set-Up: Put players in two groups, one stationed in center field throwing to home plate and the other group stationed in center field throwing to the right field line. Put a bucket at home plate for group one and a screen on the foul line for group two, as illustrated in Figure 3.10. A coach is positioned by each target with fungos.

Directions: Coach hits with a fungo and athletes throw at their respective targets and then rotate to the opposite line.

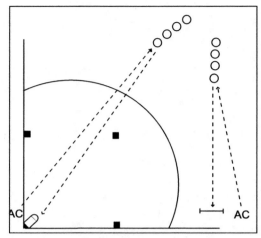

Figure 3.10. Target throwing drill

❑ Communication Drill

Set-Up: An assistant coach is positioned down the first-base line with a screen. Two groups of outfielders are in left center field and right center field.

Directions: The coach hits fly balls between the fielders. One outfielder should call for the ball and the other fielder should back her up. The fielder then quickly throws the ball into the screen next to the coach. Players rotate lines.

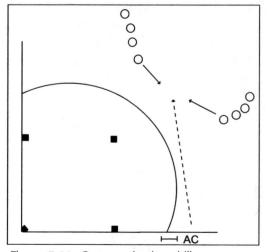

Figure 3.11. Communication drill

Pitchers

Pitching is the best defense a team can possess and good pitchers are a blessing. It is so important that you should get videos and books dedicated solely to this skill. The following videos from UCLA's 2003 Championship-winning coach Sue Enquist and Cal State Fullerton's Dee Dee Weiman are recommended.

• *Pitching Mechanics* – Offers softball players and coaches at all competitive levels an invaluable instructional tool for better understanding the key mechanical factors involved in pitching effectively. In an easy-to-understand and apply manner, coaches Enquist and Weiman break down the fundamental building blocks of sound softball pitching and detail how each block should be performed. Among the topics covered are: Wrist snap, release and follow-through, arm circle, legs, release and finish, the stride, and pre-pitch motion and feet positioning.

• *Pitching Drills* – Presents a series of proven drills that are designed to improve the fundamentals and techniques involved in pitching effectively. In an easy-to-understand and apply manner, the video explains and shows how each drill should be performed. Covers wrist-snap drills, weighted ball progressions, leg drive, walk-through, distance and six-minute speed drills.

• *Advanced Pitches and Drills* – Provides a thorough review of the fundamentals and techniques involved in throwing five specific pitches—the change-up, knuckle ball, rise ball, curve ball, and drop ball. Coaches Enquist and Weiman present these techniques in an easy-to-understand and apply manner, and also cover guidelines and drills for teaching each type of pitch. Includes additional information on alternative change-up, backdoor change-up, rise ball progressions, and more.

• *Mental Side of Pitching* – Examines the mental aspects of pitching effectively and offers advice and guidelines on how players can best deal with the "mental game" involved with pitching. With detailed clarity and insight, the video reviews each phase of the "mental game" and explains how players can

develop mental toughness, a positive attitude, and the ability to handle pressure. Covers confidence, proper perspective, leadership, setting goals, staying focused, dealing with failure, and much more.

Team Drills

Team drills should focus on game situations. Your substitutes should be as knowledgeable as your starters, so it is important that they get plenty of practice as well.

Offense

Offensively, work on the little things that add up to advancing runners and scoring runs.

❏ First-and-third Drill

Set-Up: Have half the team at third base and half the team at first base. Pitcher is positioned in the circle with catcher at home plate. Refer to Figure 3.12.

Directions: As the pitcher throws in, the runner at first steals and slows to get in a rundown. The third base runner reads the defensive player for the best jump possible. Players rotate from first to third base.

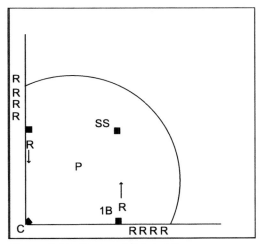

Figure 3.12. First-and-third drill

❏ Score 'Em Drill

Set-Up: Half the team at third and half the team hitting at home plate from a pitching machine.

Directions: The coach presents scenarios and goals the hitters and runners should accomplish.

- "The infield is playing in": The batter is to hit a fly ball and score the run. If the ball is hit on the ground, the runner does not go.

- "The infield is playing back": The batter is to put the ball on the ground to score the run. For example, a weak ground ball to the short stop should score the run.

- "Squeeze play": The hitter should get the bunt down to score the run.

Variations:

- Replace the pitching machine with live pitching.

- If a person is not scored, the hitter should sprint to the right field fence and back and the runner on third base should sprint to the left field fence and back.

❑ Short Game Drill

Set-Up: All team members at home plate and a batting practice pitcher or machine.

Directions: Players must execute each of the following to advance a runner from base to base.

- Hit and run – Batter hits the ball on the ground. Variation: Add a base runner.

- Bunting game – Batter bunts the ball on the ground.

- Slash – Batter fake bunts and then hits the ball on the ground. Variation: Have coach playing third base. If coach charges, player pulls bunt back and slashes. If coach stays back, player bunts.

- Right side hitting – Player hits the ball on the ground to the right side of the field.

Defense

Work on defending the bunt, rundowns, pop fly priorities, short and long alignments (relays and cutoffs), first-and-third defense, etc. Also focus on improving your team's ability to communicate and play together. The fundamental drills series allows you to cover a great deal of material while keeping everyone involved.

❑ Fundamental Drills Series

Drill #1 – *Infielders and catchers*: Force plays at home plate. Coach at home plate hits ground balls to infielders playing in for the force play at the plate. Infielders throw to catcher, who throws to first base for the double play. *Outfielders*: In right field working on fence communication. One line of outfielders in right, the other group in right center. If one fielder calls for the ball, the off fielder tells her where to throw the ball.

Drill #2 – *Catchers and first basemen*: Catchers fielding bunted balls and throwing to the first baseman. Catcher rolls out bunted ball. First baseman takes throws at first base, yelling "inside" or "outside." *Shortstops and second basemen*: Communication on ground ball around base. Coach hitting from in front of pitcher's mound. *Outfielders*: In right field going back on fly balls. Coach throwing the ball. *Third basemen*: Fielding pop fly balls at dugout and fence. Coach throwing ball to third basemen.

Drill #3 – *First basemen*: Coach hitting balls to either side of first basemen to find and increase optimum range. *Catchers and third basemen*: Catchers fielding bunted balls third-base side and throwing to third base. Third basemen charging and then going back to base properly. *Shortstop, second basemen, and outfielders*: Fly ball communication. Coach hitting fly balls from behind the mound.

Drill #4 – *Pitchers, first basemen, second basemen, and catchers*: Ground ball communication on ball hit to right side of the infield. Catcher backing up play at first base. Coach hits ground balls from third-base side. *Shortstop and third basemen*: Ground ball communication with runner forced from second base. Coach hits ground balls from first-base side. *Outfielders*: In deep center field on warning track, charging ground balls. Coach hits ground balls from second base.

Drill #5 – *Pitchers, catchers, and third basemen*: Bunt communication on bunt to third-base side. Catcher will tell fielder where to fake the throw. Coach rolls out bunted ball. Pitchers fake pitch to the plate. *First basemen and second basemen*: Ground ball communication on ball to right side of the infield. Coach hitting from first-base side of home plate. *Outfielders*: Line drive communication. Outfielders line up in center field and left center. Coach is hitting line drives from behind shortstop position. *Shortstops*: Working on short hops. Partner up and throw balls in the dirt to each other.

Drill #6 – *Shortstops, second basemen, and pitchers*: Comeback double plays. Second basemen and shortstop alternate taking throw from pitcher. *Catchers, first basemen, and third basemen*: Pickoffs. Alternate throwing to third and first. Work on giving the proper sign. *Outfielders*: In right field, fielding ground balls going to the left and right and setting up to throw. Coach is hitting from deep second base.

Drill #7 – *Catchers and third basemen*: Communication on pop-ups between third base and home plate. Coach is hitting from home plate. *Left fielders, center fielders, shortstops, and second basemen*: Throwing behind the runner rounding second base. Coach is hitting balls to outfielders in front of second base. *Right fielders and first basemen*: Ground balls to right field and throw to first. Coach is hitting ground balls from around the pitching circle.

Drill #8 – *First basemen and third basemen*: First basemen fielding bunts and throwing to third base. Third basemen work on getting back to the base. Coach is hitting bunts from third-base side of home plate. *Outfielders*: Fence work. Picking up ball at fence and hitting relay person. Work on no step prior to throw. *Catchers, second basemen, and shortstops*: Catcher throws to second base. Second basemen and shortstops alternate taking throws from catcher. Catcher works on good footwork and quickness. (Note: This drill is a good opportunity to time the catchers' throws.) Second basemen and shortstops work on snap tag.

Drill #9 – *Right fielders, second basemen, and first basemen*: Pop fly priorities. Coach is hitting from left-handed batter's box. *Left fielders, third basemen, shortstops, and center fielders*: Pop fly priorities. Coach is hitting from right-handed batter's box. *Catchers*: Blocking balls in the dirt. Working on proper techniques.

Drill #10 – *Pitchers and catchers*: Covering home plate on a wild pitch or passed ball. Catcher goes back to backstop for throw to pitcher. *First basemen*: Taking bad throws at first base. Coach is throwing from behind the pitching circle. *Outfielders, second basemen, shortstops, and third basemen*: Long alignments. Relays with play at third base. Coach is hitting ball from behind second base.

Drill #11 – *Outfielders*: Long catch. Trying to throw the ball as far and as high as they can. *First basemen, catchers, and third basemen*: Pop-up priorities. Communication in front of home plate. Coach is hitting the ball up at home plate. Second basemen and shortstops: Working on flips and tosses for double plays. Fake the throw to first base.

Drill #12 – *Catchers and pitchers*: Framing. *First basemen and shortstops*: Working on the 3-6-3 double play. Coach hitting from the third-base side. Outfielders: Quarterbacks. Coach hitting fly balls from the right field line. *Third basemen and second basemen*: Fielding short hops.

❑ Rundown Drill #1

Set-Up: Have a line of infielders at second base and third base. Coach is positioned in front of second base and a line of runners is behind second base, as illustrated in Figure 3.13.

Directions: The coach tosses a ball behind the runner to Infielder 1. Infielder 1 runs towards the runner, who is committed to running to third base. As the runner reaches the halfway point between the bases, Infielder 1 throws to Infielder 2, who is moving towards the runner. Infielder 2 chases the runner back to second base and either tags the runner or tosses the ball to the next infielder for the tag play.

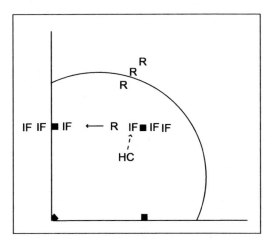

Figure 3.13. Rundown drill #1

❏ **Rundown Drill #2**

Set-Up: A group of runners at first base with all infielders in their defensive positions. Refer to Figure 3.14.

Directions: The drill starts with the pitcher pitching the ball to the catcher. As she releases the ball, the runner at first base should take a big lead. The second baseman should then run hard to first base to receive a throw from the catcher. The shortstop then runs towards the runner to receive a throw from the second baseman. The shortstop should then chase the runner back to first base, trying to tag her out. If she cannot apply a tag, she should throw the ball to the first baseman for the tag play.

Variation: Drill could be done with a pick at third base involving 3B, SS, C, or P.

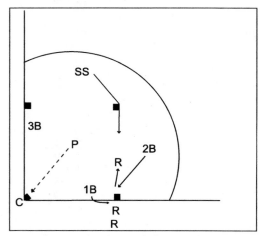

Figure 3.14. Rundown drill #2

❏ Pop Fly Priority Drill

Set-Up: Have a full team stationed in their defensive positions but add an extra center fielder. Two coaches with fungos should be stationed on either side of home plate. Divide the field as illustrated in Figure 3.15.

Directions: Coach 1 hits balls to the left side of the field, working on communication and priorities. Coach 2 hits balls to the right side of the field, also working on communication and priorities.

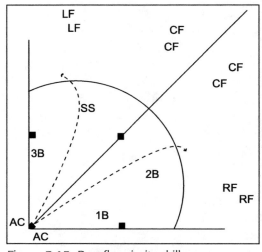

Figure 3.15. Pop fly priority drill

❏ Twenty-one Perfect Plays

Set-Up: Starters in field in defensive positions with no pitcher. Have a tee at home plate with the rest of the team hitting.

Directions: The object of the drill is to get 21 outs or perfect plays. For example, a base hit to center field that is cleanly fielded and thrown to second base is considered a perfect play although no out is made. Hitters advance normally. Clear the bases after a third out. If an error is made when the score is below 13, the score drops to zero; otherwise, it drops to 13. Once 21 perfect plays are made, switch fielders with hitters.

Variations:

• Fielders will only rotate after 21 actual outs, rather than counting perfect plays in the score.

- When they reach 18 perfect plays, require the next three points to be actual outs. Emphasize that they need these last three outs to win a game.

❏ Miscellaneous Team Drill #1

Set-Up: Starting infield in defensive positions, runners at home, coach with bucket of balls and fungo.

Directions: Coach hits ball to infielders. Infield must score nine points (or more) before the runners score six points. Infielders get one point for each out. Runners score points on fielding errors or by successfully reaching first base.

Variations:

- The infielders must get two outs to score one point.
- Put runners on different bases.
- Give runners a four-point (or more) lead.

❏ Miscellaneous Team Drill #2

Set-Up: All outfielders at left field foul line and runners at home plate. A bucket of balls is placed in shallow center field.

Directions: Outfielders must throw the runner out at second base. On the coach's signal, runners take off and the first outfielder runs to pick up a ball. The fielder attempts to throw the runner out at second base. Outfielders get a point for every out. Runners get a point for successfully reaching second base. Play to 10 or 15 points.

Variations:

- Move runners to first base and make the play at third.
- Move runners to second base and make the play at home.
- Move the bucket to the outfield fence and work on cutoffs and relays.
- Give the runners a five-point lead.

Batting Practice

Hitting is the most important part of the game, so great emphasis should be placed on it during practice. This component of practice focuses on the skill of hitting, but drills should incorporate defensive and base running skills as well. Having one hitter taking 20 swings while everyone else is shagging in the field wastes valuable practice time.

❏ Five-Minute Hitting

Set-Up: Every defensive position is filled. Other players in groups of two.

Directions: Player 1 of Group 1 is in the batter's box hitting. The group has five minutes to hit. Player 1 continues to hit as long as she is hitting the ball hard. If not, then Player 1 rotates with Player 2. Emphasis is placed on competing rather than just taking swings. As the hitters put the ball in play, the defense is live. For example, if the shortstop fields the ball, she throws to first as if a runner was approaching.

Variations:

- Put a "ghost" runner at first base for fielder's work (i.e., throw to second to make the out).
- Put actual runners on base.
- Idle groups can be at other hitting stations (e.g., soft toss and tee work into a screen).

❏ Four-Group Hitting

Set-Up: Divide the team into four groups: IF (1B, 2B, 3B, SS); C, OF (LF, CF, RF); IF; C, OF.

Directions: Rotate the groups through defense, hitting, and base running stations as illustrated in Figure 3.16.

❏ Hitting Circuit – two players at each station (Figure 3-17)

Station 1 – Live hitting
Station 2 – Shag
Station 3 – Shag
Station 4 – One-armed soft toss
Station 5 – Tee drills
Station 6 – Bunting
Station 7 – Strength
Station 8 – Tunnel with pitching machine

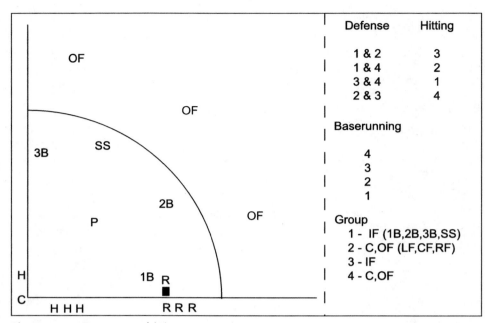

Figure 3.16. Four-group hitting

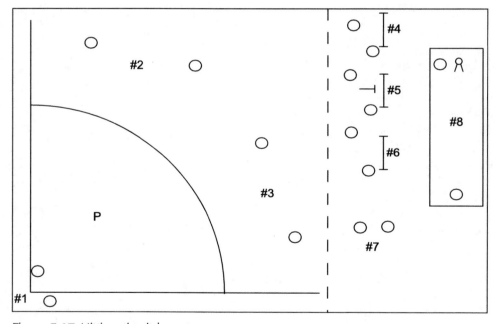

Figure 3.17. Hitting circuit layout

Conditioning

Conducting a well-run, quick-paced practice will provide plenty of conditioning for your athletes. This component of practice should focus on putting pressure on your players by making some team conditioning contingent on performance. The conditioning period is also a time to improve your team's mental toughness. It's a daily reminder that they are capable of more than they realize.

❑ Foul Poles

Set-Up: Coach at each foul pole, groups of two or three positioned at a foul pole.

Directions: Players run in groups of two or three from foul pole to foul pole on the warning track in 20 seconds.

❑ Quarterbacks

Set-Up: Players line up at the right field foul line. Every player has a ball and glove. A coach is positioned in center field. A cone is on the left field line.

Directions: One at a time, a player runs to the coach and tosses the ball to the coach. The coach then tosses the ball, leading the runner and requiring them to sprint, catch the ball, sprint around the cone, and jog back to the end of the line. Refer to Figure 3.18.

Variation: After 10 minutes, the team must catch five in a row to end the drill.

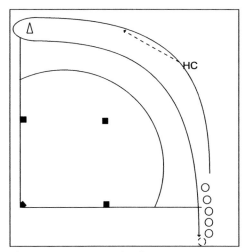

Figure 3.18. Quarterbacks

❑ Road to Happiness

Set-Up: All players lined up at home plate.

Directions: Players hit the following sequence: Four base hits (two straight through and two with a turn), three doubles, two triples, one home run.

❑ Two-Base Race

Set-Up: Split the team into two groups. Group 1 is at home plate while Group 2 is at second base.

Directions: Player 1 from each group goes on the coach's signal. When Player 1 hits the second bag, the next teammate goes. The losing team runs, does push-ups, etc.

Bad Weather Alternatives

Whether it's raining, sleeting, or snowing, you should always be prepared to have practice. Modify drills for the gym and be sure to request permission to use the gym early in the school day. In case you aren't able to use the gym, take the players into a classroom and go over long and short alignments, bunt defense, and other general defensive strategy. You might also consider watching game film or an instructional video.

Master Practice Outline

Write down all of your favorite drills on 3x5 index cards and keep them in a file. Then, write all of your favorite drills for each component of practice and make a master practice outline to be used as a quick reference sheet. As a result, you won't have to hunt or browse through drill books to find what you like, and you can periodically go to your file box for new drills. Use the reference sheet illustrated in Figure 3.19 when you fill out your daily practice schedule.

The Daily Practice Schedule

Post the practice schedule daily in an area where your players can have easy access to it. Outside your classroom, in the locker room, or at your field are all places that will give the players the opportunity to mentally prepare themselves for each practice session. A professional-looking, well-organized practice schedule will show your players that what they are doing wasn't just slapped together five minutes before the practice starts. Try to keep each

MASTER PRACTICE OUTLINE		
FUNDAMENTALS		
HITTING	**BASE RUNNING**	**CATCHERS**
1. Soft Toss	1. Take Two Drill	1. Blocking Drill
2. Tee Drill	2. Stop Watch	2. Framing Drill
3. Bunting Drill	3. Ball in Dirt	3. Pop Up's
4. Hitting Circuit	4. Signs Drill	4. Bunt Drill
PITCHING	5. Sliding Drills	5. Steal Defense Drill
1. Bunt Drill		
2. Weekly Practice Prgm		
INFIELDER'S	**OUTFIELDER'S**	**CONDITIONING**
1. Star Drill	1. Quick Throw Drill	1. Foul Poles
2. Short Hop Drill	2. Fence Drill	2. Quarterbacks
3. Throwing Drill	3. Diving Drill	3. Road to Happiness
4. Pop Up Drills	4. Target Throwing	4. Two Base Race
5. 2B/SS Fielding Drill	5. Communication Drill	5. etc.
TEAM DRILLS		**BATTING PRACTICE**
OFFENSE	**DEFENSE**	1. Four Group Hitting
1. 1st and 3rd Drill	1. Fundamental Series	2. Five Min. Hitting
2. Score 'Em Drill	2. Rundown Drills	3. Hitting Circuit
3. Short Game Drill	3. Pop Fly Priority Drill	4. etc.
4. etc.	4. 21 Perfect Plays	5. etc.

Figure 3.19. Drill reference sheet

drill or activity within the allotted time and, in an effort to keep your practice moving, keep each drill to 15 minutes or less.

Include space for the daily schedule, announcements, assigned groups, daily quotes, coaching points, and drill diagrams. Each day, make enough copies for all the coaches and managers, as well as one copy to be posted. Also file a copy each day so that in future years you can look back and see what was successful and what was not. A few sample practice schedule forms are illustrated in Figures 3.20, 3.21, and 3.22.

PRACTICE SCHEDULE - FIRST WEEK EXAMPLE

DATE: _____February 1, 2004_____   PRACTICE #: ___1____
TIME:_____3:15 pm _____   OPPONENT: _____

ANNOUNCEMENTS:

1. Pictures today at lunch - 12:00 at the field.

2. It all starts today...Practice like a champion.

THOUGHT OF THE DAY:

"Life doesn't require that we be the best, only that we give our best."

COMPETE ◆ FOCUS ◆ BELIEVE

EARLY OUTS: Corner Infielders (3:00)

MINUTES	TIME	DRILL	COMMENTS
5	3:15	Team Meeting	Set Tone
15	3:20	Jog and Agilities	
20	3:35	Throwing Program	1) One Knee 2) Isolate Feet 3)Long Catch 4) Target
15	3:55	Individual Defense	IF-GB's, short hops OF-GB's/FB's
10	4:10	Intro to Rundowns	Two line drill
10	4:20	Intro to Pop Fly Priorities	2 groups: 1)3B,SS,LF,CF 2)1B,2B,RF,CF
45	4:30	Hitting Circuit	6 stations
20	5:15	Team Offense	1)Bunt 2)Slash 3)Right Side
15	5:35	Conditioning - Around 1st	1)Out of the box 2)Through bag 3)Taking a turn

● PURSUING VICTORY WITH HONOR ●

Figure 3.20. Practice day in the first week

PRACTICE SCHEDULE - POST-SEASON EXAMPLE

DATE: __April 15, 2004_____   PRACTICE #: _____

TIME: _____3:15_____   OPPONENT: _____

ANNOUNCEMENTS:

1. Tomorrow - Dismissed at 1:40. Bus leaves at 2:00. Road uniforms.

2. Practice like a champion - deserve to win tomorrow!

THOUGHT OF THE DAY:

"The quality of a person's life is in direct proportion to their commitment to excellence." - Vince Lombardi

COMPETE ◆ FOCUS ◆ BELIEVE

EARLY OUTS: Jessica, Jenna, Desi, Britney - Base hit bunting 3:00

MINUTES	TIME	DRILL	COMMENTS
5	3:15	Team Meeting	"New Season"
15	3:20	Jog and Agilities	Include Jumps off pitcher
15	3:35	Team Defense vs. Off	Off-create situations (bunt,steal,1/3,squeeze,etc)
60	3:50	Batting Practice	
10	4:50	Team Offense	Squeeze, bunt & run

● PURSUING VICTORY WITH HONOR ●

Figure 3.21. Post-season workout

PRACTICE SCHEDULE - BAD WEATHER EXAMPLE

DATE: __March 12, 2004__

TIME: _____6:00_____

PRACTICE #: _____

OPPONENT: _____

ANNOUNCEMENTS:

1. Meet in the gym - Practice uniform and running shoes.

2. Great job yesterday!! Keep up the good work.

THOUGHT OF THE DAY:

"Ability may get you to the top, but it takes character to keep you there."

-- John Wooden

COMPETE ♦ FOCUS ♦ BELIEVE

EARLY OUTS: None

MINUTES	TIME	DRILL	COMMENTS
5	6:00	Team Meeting	Indoor exectations: no talking, focus
15	6:05	Jog and Agilities	
15	6:20	Throwing Program	
15	6:35	Individual Defense	IF - knee drills w/paddles, short hops
			OF - footwork, P and C - bullpin
5	6:50	Bunt Defense	Half speed, no runners, OF bunting
10	6:55	Offensive Special Plays	Walk through
45	7:05	Hitting Circuit	8 stations
15	7:45	Conditioning	

● PURSUING VICTORY WITH HONOR ●

Figure 3.22. Practice day in bad weather

Other Practice Concerns

First Game Preparation

As you prepare for your first game, explain to your less experienced players the pre-game procedures, including pre-game infield, national anthem behavior, effort required running in and out of the dugout, various game duties, and other rules and procedures. Practice these things during an intersquad scrimmage. This step will help eliminate confusion on game day.

Pre-Game Fielding Series

Before taking the field, the team should have worked through the throwing program and some hitting drills. You can choose from many different drill series for pre-game warm-up. The following illustrates one possible basic pre-game routine:

❑ Starting Outfield (on field with starting infield)

• Fly balls and grounders to each outfielder and thrown to 2B and 3B.

• Fly balls and grounders to each outfielder and thrown to cutoff, then relayed to home plate.

❑ Starting Infield (outfielders with other coach fielding fly balls)

• Star drill x 2 with reverse

• Ground balls to each infielder and thrown to first base, second base, third base, and home plate.

• Turn two (SS to 1B and 2B to 1B) x 2-3

• Have pitcher join field and practice bunt coverage.

❑ Coming In

Hit to each fielder and have her throw to the catcher and then run off the field.

National Anthem Behavior

A good coach pays attention to every detail of the game, including how to stand and act during the national anthem. If you are the home team, position players in groups as illustrated in Figure 3.23. Each player should stand the same way. For example, feet together, right hand on heart, left hand behind back.

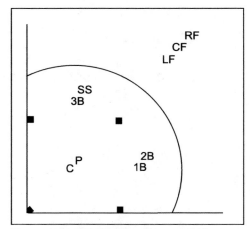

Figure 3.23. National anthem positions

Running In and Out of the Dugout

Practice running in and out of the dugout. Effort is what should be emphasized. Players should run as hard as they can out to the field and take their positions, and players should also run to the dugout as hard as they can. When coming to bat, you may have the team huddle up to do a cheer or talk strategy before entering the dugout. You want to beat the other team in every aspect of the game.

Game Duties

The following additional game duties are sometimes overlooked. Assign a player to each one:

• Warming up the off outfielder.

• Getting a ball to the center fielder.

• Getting a ball to the first baseman.

• Warming up the pitcher between innings.

• Managing charts (see Chapter 8 for charts to use during the game).

• Having the batter's glove ready in case she makes the last out of the inning.

Miscellaneous Rules and Procedures

- Players should not leave the dugout to talk or to go to the concession stand.

- When the team is on offense, everyone should be up in the dugout cheering.

- No horseplay in the dugout.

- All players should be focused.

- Bats and helmets should *never* be thrown.

- The player who makes the last out of the inning should give her helmet and gloves to the nearest base coach.

Communication

Players must have ongoing, clear communication during all defensive and offensive situations to prevent such occurrences as a dropped ball. Emphasize communication in practice so it becomes second nature in a game situation. Lack of communication is unacceptable!

A Final Thought

Although games are about your players, practice is about you, the coach, and what you can bring to each practice that will help your team get better. The drills you assign and the energy in which you present them make the difference. A team that pays the price is the team that deserves the rewards. Does this always happen? Certainly not, but it's all about pursuing greatness and striving to be the best team you can.

Photo: Leslie Scott

Fundamental Skills and Strategies

Hitting

The Bat

Each player should choose a bat that allows her to create optimal bat-head speed. Instead of choosing the lightest bat available (a common mistake), coaches should consider a combination of factors, including swing mechanics, grip, and bat size and weight. Swinging the heaviest bat she feels comfortable with allows the batter more opportunity to drive the ball with more distance and velocity.

An increasing amount of quality bats exist on the market, with all types of specifications and technologies. A great way for a coach to shop for bats is to watch college softball games and watch the ball come off the bat. You'll see a definite difference from bat to bat. Strong, bigger girls should look for a bat in the −8 to −9 range, while smaller, less powerful girls should work with a −9 to −10 model. Length is less of an issue. Look for a length that feels comfortable and allows for plate coverage.

For high school players, a bat 32″ to 34″ is standard. A lot of the major colleges and players are moving more and more towards the end-loaded, smaller sweet spot bats, as opposed to the bottle bat models that were a softball standard for years. The end-loaded models allow for more bat-head speed, as well as more power off the bat.

The Grip

Keep in mind the following points when teaching the grip:

- Align the door-knocking knuckles.

- Grip the bat with both hands close together.

- Keep hands relaxed but firm.

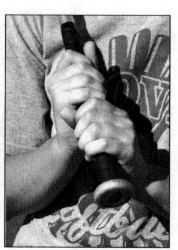

Figure 4.1. Bat grip

The Stance and Ready Position

A lot of great hitters through the years have been able to hit using a variety of different stances. It doesn't matter too much how you stand at the plate as long as you are comfortable. Put your players in an athletic, workable stance. Try to get players as close to a squared stance as possible. A closed or open stance, while at times successful, creates other problems for the hitter. For example, a hitter with a closed stance normally will hit the ball down well, but will often have trouble with a pitch up and in. Being in a squared, athletic position puts the hitter in the best, most consistent starting point and will make it easier for both of you to make minor adjustments to the swing as the year progresses. Refer to Figure 4.2.

Figure 4.2. Batting stance

Location in the Batter's Box

Depending on what and how the pitcher is throwing, the location the batter sets up in in the batter's box will vary. If the pitcher is throwing everything hard or her out pitch is the rise ball, backing up in the box will help because it allows the hitter more reaction time. If the pitcher is throwing a lot of off-speed pitches or pitches that break late, moving up in the box allows the hitter to make contact with the ball before it breaks.

The Swing

The swing has five components:

The Launch and Load Position

- Weight should be evenly distributed, with good balance, knees flexed, and hips square to the plate.

- Head should be over the center of the body.

- Hands should be high with wrists cocked and the bat at a 45-degree angle.

- Stride foot is down at a 90-degree angle with a firm front side completing the launch.

The Beginning of the Swing

- Weight transfers to the center with hips square to the plate.

- The back leg slightly cocks forward with a quarter turn of the back foot.

- Front leg remains firm to create resistance.

The Swing Path

- The hips start to turn slightly.

- The elbows move toward the contact zone, slightly in front of the hips.

- The back elbow is tight to the body in a 45-degree angle.

- Wrists are cocked.

- Hands are leading the barrelhead in palm-up and palm-down position.

- Hands are higher than the barrel.

- Head holds still, with weight balanced.

- Front arm is slightly bent.

The Contact

- Weight is forward, but not outside the lead leg.
- Back elbow extends.
- The wrist snaps.
- Front leg is firm and front foot is closed.
- Back leg and hips drive forward.

The Follow-through

- Head remains still and finishes over back shoulder.
- Stride foot "opens," but only after completion of the swing.
- Arms follow through the natural progression of the swing, sometimes finishing low but preferably finishing high (based on swing path and pitch location).

Top Three Hitting Faults and Corrections

Hitting Fault #1: Casting of the Hands

This error is caused by the elbow breaking first, which "throws" the hands out in front, creating a long, slower swing.

Hitting Fault #2: Opening the Front Foot on the Stride

When a hitter opens the front foot on the stride, it throws the hitter off balance. The batter should stride with a closed front foot.

Hitting Fault #3: Swinging Late

Far too many young hitters start their swing too late. The launch and load components should happen prior to the ball being released.

Knowing Your Opponent

A good hitter is a prepared hitter. During game preparation, a hitter should already be aware of the pitches that are thrown for strikes based on the pitcher pattern chart (see Chapter 7, Figure 7.3).

On Deck

Before the batter gets on deck, she should be mentally preparing for her at-bat while in the dugout. When on deck, she should focus on the situation:

- How many outs are there?
- Where are the runners?
- What is the pitcher's pattern?
- Where are the defensive weaknesses?
- How is the defense aligned?

Taking Signs

As a batter enters the box, she should look at the coach as soon as possible to get the sign and get on with the game.

The Count

- No count – The hitter should look for the pitcher's best pitch, one she throws for a strike.
- Two-strike count (0-2) – The pitcher may throw a "waste" pitch down and away or a rise pitch to get the batter to "fish" for the ball.
- One- and two-ball count (1-0 or 2-0) – This situation is the best hitting count and allows for aggressive hitting.
- Three-ball count (3-0)
  - ❏ When to hit
    - ✓ Your top hitter is at the plate with runners on base.
    - ✓ The hitter has been "hot."
    - ✓ The hitter is disciplined.
    - ✓ You have a big lead in the game.
  - ❏ When to take
    - ✓ A weaker hitter is at the plate.

✓ You are behind in the game.

✓ The batter is leading off an inning.

- Full count (3-2) – The pitcher will throw her best pitch to get a strike, so this situation also allows for aggressive hitting.

The Situation

- Runner on second and no outs – The batter should hit to the right side of the infield to attempt to move the runner.

- Runner on third and less than two outs – With the infield playing in, the batter should hit a fly ball deep enough to score a tagging runner.

- Runner on first and no outs – The batter should attempt to move the runner into scoring position either by bunting, drawing a walk, or getting a base hit.

Bunting

The Grip

When bunting, the batter should hold the bat in a way that allows for the best bat control. The standard way of accomplishing this control is to choke up slightly with the bottom hand and pinch the lower part of the bat's barrel with the top hand.

The Stance

When attempting any type of bunt, the batter should position herself in the front of the box to minimize the amount of foul territory in front of her. The standard ways to set up for a bunt are the pivot and the square-up.

Pivot – This method is the easiest and safest to teach. The batter should simply pivot on the back foot, squaring her chest to the pitcher. Make sure she bends at the knees as illustrated in Figure 4.3.

Square-up – This method requires the batter to bring forward her back foot, which will completely

Figure 4.3. The pivot

square up the feet, knees, waist, chest, shoulder, and head towards the pitcher. Again, make sure she bends her knees (see Figure 4.4).

Figure 4.4. The square-up

Making Contact

When attempting to get the ball down on a bunt, the most important thing is to keep the bat at an angle. The bat should remain close to a 45-degree angle throughout the bunt attempt. This angle will force the ball down off the bat. In order to achieve this angle on a low pitch, the batter should bend at the knees, not lower the bat head.

Types of Bunts

Sacrifice Bunt

When attempting a sacrifice bunt, the batter is "giving herself up" for the good of the team. Therefore, the element of surprise and getting to first base quickly are not priorities—advancing the runner is. The batter should make sure she attempts at only strikes and deadens the ball about 5 to 10 feet in front of home plate.

Drag Bunt

Unlike the sacrifice bunt, the drag bunt is about getting on base. Once again, the batter should only attempt at strikes and the ball should be placed down either baseline. To determine which line to choose, simply look at where both the first and third baseman are positioned. Whoever is further back should be where the drag bunt is directed.

Push Bunt

As with the drag bunt, the push bunt is used in an attempt to reach base. The idea of the push bunt is to bunt the ball hard enough to get it past the corners and pitcher and force either the shortstop or second baseman to make the play.

Suicide Squeeze

Unlike all the other bunts mentioned in this section, the suicide squeeze bunt requires the bunter to make contact with any pitch—ball or strike. The goal of the suicide squeeze play is to score a runner from third by catching the defense off guard. Because of the surprise factor of the play, the batter should not react to the pitch for as long as possible. With a good jump by the runner at third, the batter needs only to get the ball down in fair territory for the base runner to score.

Safety Squeeze

When executing the safety squeeze, the bunter does not have to successfully bunt the ball. If she does make contact, the runner waits for the throw to be made to first. Once the ball leaves the fielder's hand, the runner breaks for home plate.

Run and Bunt

When the base runner is stealing, the hitter must bunt the ball whether it is a ball or a strike. The runner should be looking to advance to third, either on a well-placed bunt or an uncovered base (i.e., the third baseman fields the bunt).

Fielding

Ready Position

The fielder stands on the balls of the feet for a good foundation, with the feet about shoulder-width apart and the knees slightly bent. The corner positions of the infield should set up in a low position to help with reaction time, whereas the middle infielders should stand more upright.

Moving to the Ball

The fielder should read the ball off the bat. Because of the speed of the game of softball, a player must take a more direct angle to the ball. Coach her to get in front of each ground ball.

Ground Balls

Infielders

The fielder's glove should be out in front (not under her body) and in a good ready position.

Figure 4.5. "Do or die" fielding

Figure 4.6. One-knee method

Outfielders

With runners in scoring position, an outfielder should work on the "do or die" fielding method. She should charge the ball aggressively, with the glove to the outside. She should field, step through, and throw without a hop step, as illustrated in Figure 4.5. When no runners are in scoring position, the outfielder can simply field a ground ball like an infielder. With no one on base and poor fielding conditions (wet, holes, bumpy, etc.), the outfielder can use the one-knee method (Figure 4.6).

Fly Balls

- Teach the crossover step or drop step to get behind the ball.
- Players should call for the ball loudly and clearly.

Pop-ups in the Sun

- The fielders should take note of where the sun is before the ball is put in play.

- Fielders should shade their eyes with the glove.
- Players can use special "flip-down" sunglasses.

Applying a Tag

Teach the following two concepts for applying a tag:

- Don't reach out at the runner, just let them come to you.
- Tag with two hands.

Throwing

The Throwing Motion

The basic throwing motion is a circle, as illustrated in Figure 4.7. Depending on the position, that circle either decreases or increases. The throwing arm travels from the glove, by the hip, and up to a position parallel to the ground with the ball facing away from the target. As the arm completes the circle, the hand holding the ball rotates behind the ball, with the upper arm parallel to the ground.

Figure 4.7. The throwing motion

The Follow-through

The follow-through should allow all the built-up energy to exit through the fingers. Refer to Figure 4.8.

Base Running

From Home Plate

- After taking three to five steps out of the box, the runner should find the ball to determine if the ball got through the infield.

- Everyone should run every ball out.

To First Base

- Players should run through first base on a ball hit to the infield, touching the front portion of the base.

- She should then pull up as quickly as possible and pick up the first base coach for a possible overthrow.

- Teach taking as big a turn as possible if the ball makes it through the infield, and then continuing on towards second base until the defense does something that dictates for her to stop. Runners should apply pressure.

- The runner should hit the base with the inside foot on the turn at first base.

- During the return back to first base, the runner should keep her eye on the ball, always looking for an errant throw.

- If a batted ball that reaches the outfield draws a throw to another base, she should look to take second base on the throw.

Figure 4.8. The follow-through

From Second Base

- On a ground ball to the right of the runner, she should advance to third base only after she sees the ball go by the infielders.

- On a groundball to the left or directly at the runner on second, she should advance to third base.

- If the ball is hit to right field, the athlete must rely on the third base coach for direction.

- When getting a jump from second base with two outs, the runner should angle two or three steps behind the baseline. This position gives the runner a better angle to round third base on an attempt to score.

- Base runners should always look at where the outfielders are playing. This information will help in the decision whether a ball is going to drop in or be caught, thus making it easier to score.

From Third Base

- Runners should always take a look at where the infielders are playing. This information will help in the decision whether to go home on a ground ball or to see it through.

- On any ball hit in the air, regardless of whether it's hit fair or foul, a base runner should always go back to the base to tag.

- Runners should always take their leads in foul territory.

Sliding

Bent Leg

The bent leg slide is the easiest slide to execute and the most widely used of all the slides. The bent leg slide is accomplished by forming a "4" with the legs. In other words, one leg is straight out, while the other leg is bent at a 90-degree angle under the straight leg, as illustrated in Figure 4.9.

Coaching points:

- About 90% of ground contact should be made with the buttocks. Abrasions are caused when players make unnecessary contact with their hips, knees, shins, and hands.

- Hands should be up, not on the ground.

- The bent leg slide allows the runner to run at full speed the longest, making it the fastest way to reach the base.

Figure 4.9. Bent leg slide

Hook

The hook slide is an advanced form of sliding. The hook slide is executed by sliding on either side of the base and hooking the base with an outstretched foot. This slide minimizes the amount of body surface area for the defender to tag. Refer to Figure 4.10.

Fade Away

The fade away slide is another more advanced way of sliding. Like the hook slide, the fade away diminishes the ability of the defender to apply a tag. The fade away is performed by sliding on either side of the base, while reaching for the base with an outstretched hand. See Figure 4.11.

Head First

The head first slide is another popular form of sliding. It requires the runner to dive hands and head first into the base.

Figure 4.10. Hook slide

Figure 4.11. Fade away slide

Photo: David Menedian

5

Offensive Strategy

The Batting Order

Assign your players a position in the line-up according to the following characteristics:

Lead-off

- should have good speed
- a base-stealing threat
- good on-base percentage
- good hitter
- aggressive base runner

#2 Hitter

- should have good bat control
- a good bunter
- able to hit the ball behind runners (the right side)
- should have good speed

#3 Hitter

- should be your best hitter (high average)
- run producer
- clutch hitter
- hottest hitter

#4 Hitter

- best run producer
- clutch hitter
- power hitter

#5 Hitter

- run producer
- a good hitter (average is not as important as RBIs)
- depending on the depth of your line-up, bunting might be an important characteristic

#6 Hitter

- run producer (average is not as important as RBIs)
- power hitter

#7 Hitter

- able to advance runners
- lowest-average hitter

#8 Hitter

- puts the ball in play with good bat control
- good bunting ability
- advances runners
- speed is a plus

#9 Hitter

- should have good speed
- a base-stealing threat
- good on-base percentage
- good hitter
- aggressive base runner
- good bunting ability
- "pesky" hitter

Hitting Strategies

Hit and Run

The hit-and-run is used to advance a runner to the next base. It also offers a chance, because of the movement of the infielders created by the steal, for the hitter to also reach base, creating a big rally situation.

Slash

The slash is done in a sacrifice bunt situation and is used when a defense charges the batter too aggressively.

Right-side Hitting (Hitting Behind the Runner)

A batter hits behind the runner in an effort to advance the runner to the next base. The best time to execute this strategy is with no outs and a runner on second base. Hitting the ball on the ground to the second baseman will allow your runner at second to move to third base.

Fly Ball

The ability to hit a fly ball is a valuable part of any team's offense. With a runner at third and less than two outs, a fly ball allows your offense to trade an out for a run.

Bunting Strategies

Fake Bunt

This tactic is used to get the defense moving out of position, which allows runners on base to steal the next base. It is also used to slow and distract the catcher during an attempt to throw out the base runner on a steal attempt. To execute a fake bunt, the batter assumes a bunting position and pulls the bat back as the pitched ball comes to the plate.

Bunt for a Hit

A batter bunts when trying to reach base, usually with no one on base. It is an effective way to start an inning or disrupt an effective pitcher.

Sacrifice Bunt

A player should sacrifice bunt to advance base runners. This bunt is usually executed with no outs and runners at first base, second base, or both, but it can also be used to advance your runners with one out, depending on your offensive philosophy.

Suicide Squeeze

The suicide squeeze is attempted with less than two outs and with a runner at third or runners at second and third. It can be done with bases loaded, but doing that makes it an easier play for the defense since they have a force-out at home. You can use the suicide squeeze at any point in a game regardless of the score, but you shouldn't use it with a big lead or if your team is trailing by a big margin. Consider using it when the hitter at-bat isn't generally a run-producer. In other words, if your number three hitter is at the plate, you should let her hit away to try to score the run. If your number nine hitter is at-bat, consider using the suicide squeeze to get the runner home.

Safety Squeeze

You might consider using the safety squeeze if your opponent has a more athletic infield. Unlike the suicide squeeze, with the safety squeeze you are not giving yourself up completely. Also, consider using the safety squeeze if the opponent has a weak-throwing first or second baseman. Delaying the steal will force one of the two fielders to make a play at home. The safety squeeze is used at the same point in the game as a suicide squeeze (less than two outs, runner at third, etc.).

Run and Bunt

A run-and-bunt is used to advance runners on one or more bases. This play is done with a runner at first base, second base, or both, with no outs. It can also be used with one out, depending on your philosophy. Use the run-and-bunt for two reasons:

* It gives a slower runner on base a head start when trying to advance to the next base.

* It gives a very fast and aggressive runner a chance to possibly advance two bases on the play.

The Steal

Single or Double Steal

When to use the steal:

* The runner on base is quick and a base-stealing threat.

* You have one or two outs and the lead-off or number nine hitter is at the plate. With the number nine hitter on base and the lead-off batter at-bat with two outs, it's a win-win situation, because either she steals the base and you have a runner in scoring position with a good hitter at the plate, or you have your lead-off batter to start the next inning.

* A good hitter is at the plate and is way behind in the count or has a 3-1 count.

* You're trying to get the tying or winning run into scoring position late in the game

Delayed Steal

When to delay steal:

* The other team exhibits laziness on defense. For example, the catcher lobs the ball to the pitcher and the shortstop and second baseman drop their heads (not paying attention).

* You have an aggressive base runner on base.

* After a big play and the defense is still reeling.

Strategies for Special Situations

Start of an Inning

* Try to work the pitcher deep into the count.

* Reach base with a walk, hit, or on an error.

Runner at First

* Work to advance the runner into scoring position.

* With no outs, sacrifice bunt or slash.

* With one out, use the hit-and-run or steal.

Runner on Second

* No outs — Advance the runner to third using a bunt or hit to the right side.

* One or two outs — Try to score on a single.

- One out without a run producer at the plate – Bunt.

Runner on Third

- If it's a close game and late, squeeze.

- If the defense is playing in, hit a fly ball.

- If the defense is back, hit to the shortstop or second baseman.

- Must score the runner on third with less than two outs—no excuses.

Runners on First and Second

- No outs – Advance runners using a bunt or slash.

- One or two outs – Score the runner from second by hitting to the right side.

- Your team should score at least one run this inning.

Runners on First and Third

- Force the defense to make a play on the runner at first in a rundown situation to score the runner at third.

- Use the squeeze. If the runner at third gets out, the runner at first moves to second, still giving you a runner in scoring position.

- Your team must work to score the runner at third.

Runners on Second and Third

- Good time to squeeze. If unsuccessful, you still have a runner at third.

- Runner at third automatically goes on a ground ball.

Bases Loaded

- Goal should be to score two runs.

- Look to see what the defense is giving you. If the infield is back, the hitters should put the ball on the ground and score a run. If the infield is playing up, then hitters should hit two sacrifice flies.

- Batter should not stray from the strike zone. A walk is a run.

Coaching the Bases

First Base Coach

- Know how many outs you have.

- Know the signs.

- On a play at first with a high throw that draws the first baseman off the base, the first base coach should instruct the runner whether or not to slide.

- With a runner at first, look for the second baseman on a pick play.

Third Base Coach

- Know how many outs you have.

- Know the signs.

- Know game strategies.

- With a runner at third base, look for the shortstop on a pick play.

- With a runner at second base, look for a pick play.

- With a runner at first base and the ball hit down the right field line, direct the runner what to do.

- Tell player at third base whether they go home on contact or see the ball through the infield.

Giving Signals

The most popular system used is the indicator system. The first body part you touch becomes the key. When you touch this same body part during a series, the sign that follows it will be the one indicating the tactic.

Your first task is to assign tactics to signals. For example:

- Sacrifice – right hand to ear
- Steal – left hand to buckle
- Hit-and-run – right hand rubbed down pants
- Squeeze – right hand to left arm
- Take – left hand to right wrist
- Cancel – left hand rubbed down pants

Coaching points:

- When giving signs, give them all every time and do not start or finish with what you want the athlete to do.
- Instruct players to look at you and watch the entire series of signs before looking away. Looking away too soon could tip off the opposition.
- Give signs at a pace your players can follow.
- Consider a simple method of relaying signs by where you are positioned in the coaching box or how you are standing.

The Complete Book of Baseball Signs and Plays by Stu Southworth provides an extensive collection of baseball signs and signals for every situation in a game. The book covers umpires' signals, offensive and defensive gestures, and coaching signs.

Other Considerations

Pinch Hitters

Use a pinch hitter during an important situation in a game when the hitter due up is not likely to get a specific job done (bunt, fly ball, clutch hit, etc.).

Pinch Runners

The number of good runners you have on the bench may determine how often a pinch runner is used. If you are limited to just a few, you should save them for a crucial time when the game is close.

Designated Hitter

Designated hitters are usually players whose hitting ability makes up for their lack of defensive skill. Use the designated hitter at any point in the line-up to replace your weakest hitter.

Photo: Leslie Scott

6

Defensive Strategy

General Rules of Defense

- Always keep the ball in front of you.

- Make the sure out.

- Eliminate advancing runners by throwing to the proper base.

- Prepare for all situations (late in game, trick plays, etc.).

- Be great in defending the short game.

- Keep the leadoff batter of each inning off base.

- Allow no walks.

- Don't let the opposing team's best player beat you. Utilize the intentional walk.

Player Responsibilities

Figures 6.1 to 6.31 illustrate coverage areas, cut-off responsibilities, and back-up duties for each position in some common plays. Many of these ideas are covered explicitly for each player in Chapter 4, but the diagrams in this section illustrate the "big picture" and how each player works together.

The following situations should be played as if no one is on base.

- Double to left field – runner on second and third base

- Double to center field – runner on second and third base

- Double to right field – runner on second and third base

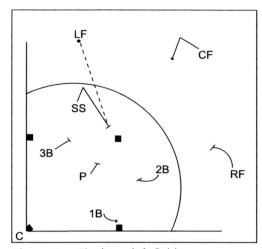

Figure 6.1. Single to left field – no one on base

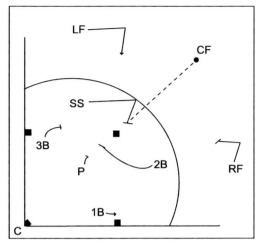

Figure 6.2. Single to center field – no one on base

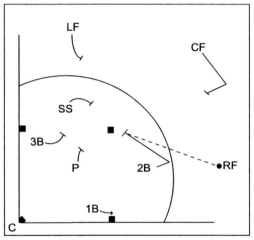

Figure 6.3. Single to right field – no one on base

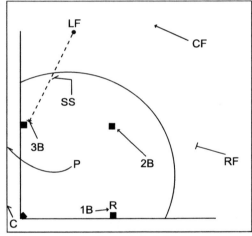

Figure 6.4. Single to left field – runner on first base

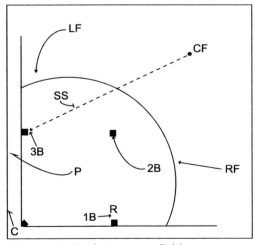

Figure 6.5. Single to center field – runner on first base

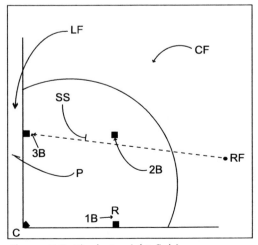

Figure 6.6. Single to right field – runner on first base

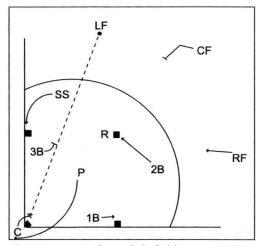

Figure 6.7. Single to left field – runner on second base

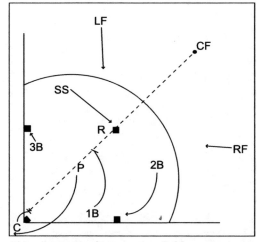

Figure 6.8. Single to center field – runner on second base

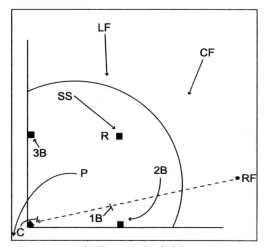

Figure 6.9. Single to right field – runner on second base

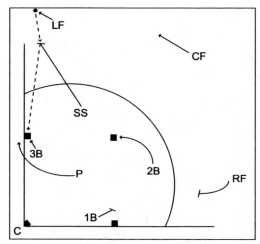

Figure 6.10. Double down left field line – no one on base

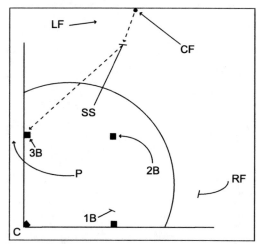

Figure 6.11. Double to left-center – no one on base

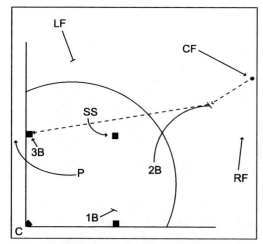

Figure 6.12. Double to right-center – no one on base

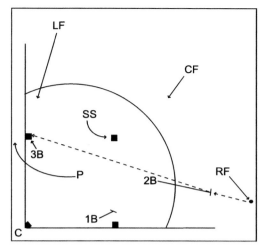

Figure 6.13. Double down right field line – no one on base

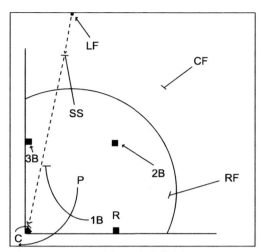

Figure 6.14. Double to left field – runner on first base

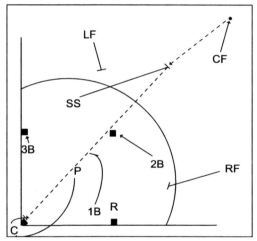

Figure 6.15. Double to center – runner on first base

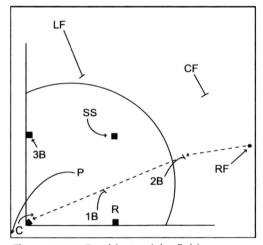

Figure 6.16. Double to right field – runner on first base

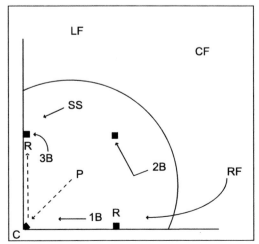

Figure 6.17. Defending the first and third situation – arm fake

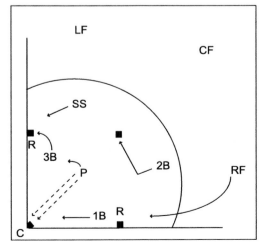

Figure 6.18. Defending the first and third situation – high throw to pitcher

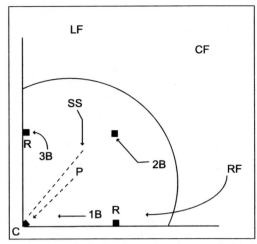

Figure 6.19. Defending the first and third situation – cut-off with shortstop

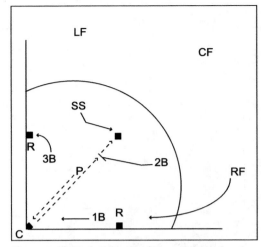

Figure 6.20. Defending the first and third situation – throw through with second baseman cut option

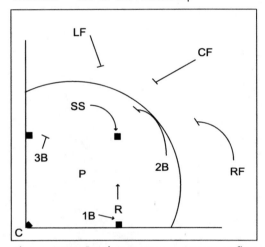

Figure 6.21. Steal coverage – runner at first – standard coverage

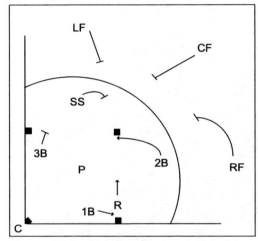

Figure 6.22. Steal coverage – runner at first – slapper/pull hitter

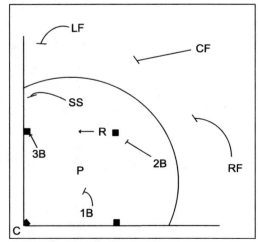

Figure 6.23. Steal coverage – runner at second – standard coverage

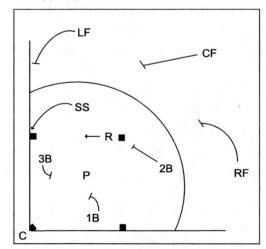

Figure 6.24. Steal coverage – runner at second – slapper

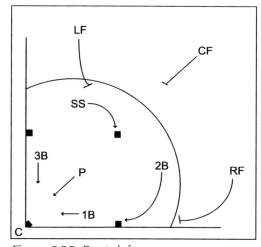

Figure 6.25. Bunt defense – no one on

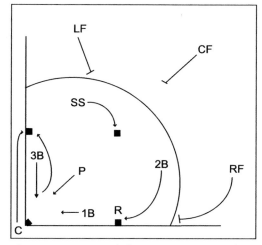

Figure 6.26. Bunt defense – runner on first

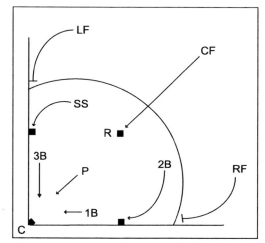

Figure 6.27. Bunt defense – runner on second

POP-UP ASSIGNMENTS		
POSITION	HAS PRIORITY OVER	DOES NOT HAVE PRIORITY OVER
C	Pitcher	1B, 3B
P	No Fielder	C, 1B, 2B, SS, 3B
1B	C, P	2B, SS, 3B, RF
2B	P, 1B	SS, All Outfielder's
SS	P, 1B, 2B, SS	All Outfielder's
3B	P, C, 1B	SS, LF
LF	All Infielder's	CF
CF	All Infielder's, LF, RF	No Fielder
RF	All Infielder's	CF

Figure 6.28. Pop-up assignment coverage

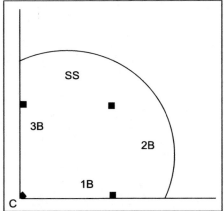

Figure 6.29. Normal infield depth

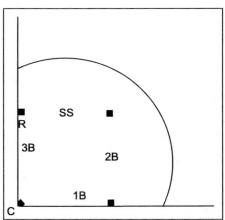

Figure 6.30. Double play depth

Figure 6.31. Infield depth – runner on third

Run-down Situations

- Player with the ball should run with the ball up by her ear.

- Players should use dart throws.

- Both defensive players must be on the same side of the base line.

- Fielders should run hard at the runner, forcing her back to the bag where she started, never to the next base.

- Players should not use arm fakes because they will mess up the timing of the play.

- The player receiving the ball should always be moving forward toward the runner.

Double Plays

- Make sure you get one out.

- Make sure your first baseman comes off the bag looking for the next play, rather than celebrating after completing a double play.

Photo: Leslie Scott

7

Scouting

Live scouting is obviously more challenging than watching a film that you can stop, pause, and rewind. You should ask an assistant or a knowledgeable friend to go with you as you scout an upcoming opponent.

General Checklist

Use the form shown in Figure 7.1 as an example of a scouting report. Gather the following information:

- Get the starting lineup, including names and numbers.

- Next to each starter, indicate strengths and weaknesses, whether she is left-handed or right-handed, and position played.

- Watch for substitutions—note who goes in for each player.

- Indicate the weaknesses of substitutes.

- Watch for hitting tendencies.

- Note where the players generally play defense.

```
TEAM SCOUTING REPORT

TEAM: _____  COACH: _____

Key Players:                     Pitchers:
_____         _____
_____         _____
_____
_____

Offensive Strategy: (first and third, steal, bunt and run, hit and run, sac, etc.)
_____
_____
_____
_____

Defensive Strategy: (backups, first and third, positioning, bunt coverage)
_____
_____
_____
_____

Hitting: (pitches preferred, singles, bunts, power, etc.)
_____
_____

Offensive Strategy: (first and third, steal, bunt and run, hit and run, sac, etc.)
_____
_____
_____
```

Figure 7.1. Team scouting report

- Find the weak link (e.g., a player who folds under pressure, doesn't hit particularly well, is tentative as a fielder, etc.).

- Note key players and their strengths (e.g., right fielder has exceptional throwing arm, lead-off batter has great speed on the bases).

Offensive Checklist

- Keep a chart for each hitter and save it for every time you see her play. Refer to Figure 7.2.

- Note how she handles special situations (e.g. bunt, hit-and-run, steals).

- Does she bat right-handed or left-handed?

- Does she have speed on the bases?

- Does she mix up where she hits the ball or is she predictable?

- Note the result of every at-bat and the pitch that was thrown if it was an out. For example, strikeout swinging on a drop ball (K drop) or thrown out at first by the second baseman hitting a curve ball (4-3 curve).

- Keep a pitcher pattern chart. Refer to Figure 7.3.

- Note which pitch is thrown ahead in the count and behind in the count.

- Determine her best pitch (rise, drop, curve, or change).

- Take the information on each hitter and fill in the player positioning chart as illustrated in Figure 7.4. Use this chart as a quick reference for defensive positioning.

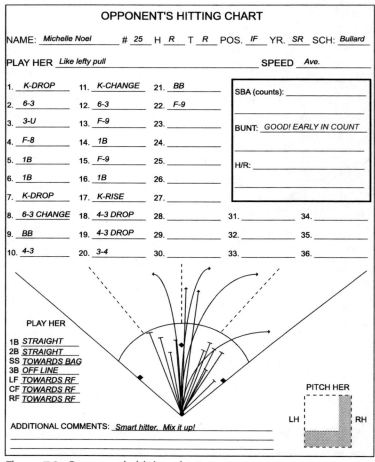

Figure 7.2. Opponent's hitting chart

PITCHER PATTERN CHART

TEAM _____ PITCHER _____ DATE _____

	first pitch	1-0 count	0-1 count	1-1 count	ahead in count 0-2, 1-2, 2-2	behind in count 2-1, 2-0, 3-0	3-2	SO
innings 1 & 2	R R R C D R C R	D D CH	R R R CH R D	D C C D	CH R R R C D R CH R	D D CH D CH	D D	R CH
innings 3 & 4	D R R C D D	D C	R R R CH	C C D CH	R R R CH CH D D R	CH D D C D C R D	D C	D R D
innings 5 thru 7	D D R R R C C R R R	D D D	R R CH CH R D R R	CH D R	R R C D R R CH R	CH D D C C R D R	D CH D	R D CH R

COMMENTS: _Ahead in count: RISE   Behind in count: DROP_

BEST PITCH: _RISE!_

KEY: RISE - R   DROP - D   CURVE - C   CHANGE - CH

Figure 7.3. Pitcher pattern chart (Used with permission from *Baseball/Softball Playbook* by Ron Polk and Donna LoPiano)

PLAYER POSITIONING CHART

OPPONENT _Mt. Pilot_ DATE _3/14/2003_

#	Player	Pos	R/L	Outfield	Infield	Comments
25	Noel, Tiffany	OF	L	to left; LF in	5-6 hole - in	speed
1	Douglas, Bailey	OF	L	to left; LF in	5-6 hole - in	speed
7	Awalt, Mary	SS	R	straight - deep	regular	don't let her beat us!
4	Scott, Claire	3B	R	straight - deep	regular	mix it up!
21	White, Norma	1B	R	deep	regular	keep it down
20	Douglas, Juliet	2B	R	straight ⟶		
22	Peterson, Juliet	P	L	to left; LF in	5-6 hole - in	slapper
10	Adair, Laurie	OF	L	to left; LF in	5-6 hole - in	speed!
24	Noel, Avery	DH	R	straight ⟶		
12	White, Peggy	PH	R	straight ⟶		
2	Wilson, Irene	PH	R	straight ⟶		

Figure 7.4. Player positioning chart

Defensive Checklist

- Note their defense on bunt situations, first-and-thirds, and backups.

- How well do the outfielders throw?

- Does the catcher have a good arm?

- Are the shortstop and second baseman alert when the ball is thrown to the pitcher?

Develop a Practice Plan

- After scouting your opponent, it's time to decide on a plan of attack. Develop a practice plan based on the following:

- Practice hitting to the weakest fielder.

- Practice hitting to the corner infielders.

- Carefully look at your opponent's lineup and practice shifts.

- Make players aware of where the ball is put in play from each player on the opposing team. Simulate these situations using your scout team.

- Have your scout team run the same coverage you expect from the opponent during special plays (bunt, first-and-third, etc.).

8

Game Day Considerations

Away Game Preparation

Uniform Management

Develop a system for handing out and collecting uniforms for an away game. Set the uniforms out about 30 minutes before departure time. After the game, each player should put her own uniform, turned inside out, into the laundry bag. The managers should be responsible for getting the uniforms on the bus and then laundered when back at school.

Travel Information

Post an itinerary so players are fully informed of when they should be released from class, when the bus leaves, and when the game starts. Also include assignments for various responsibilities, including helmet duty, ball duty, whiffle ball duty, and jacket duty. Add the starting line-up, as well, so players can begin to get into "game mode." Figure 8.1 illustrates a sample game day information sheet.

GAME DAY INFORMATION SHEET		
Opponent _____ Date _____		
Released at _____		
Bus leaves at _____ from _____		
Game starts at _____		
Helmet duty _____		
Ball duty _____		
Whiffle ball duty _____		
Jacket bag duty _____		
Starting Line-Up	Other Notes:	
1.		
2.		
3.		
4.		
5.		
6.		
7.		
8.		
9.		

Figure 8.1. Game day information sheet

Trip Items

Your managers should have a travel checklist including the following items:

- Scorebooks
- Line-up cards
- Statistics sheets
- Balls
- Bats
- Helmets
- Whiffle balls
- Water bottles/water jug and cups
- Towels
- Extra uniforms, stirrups, knee pads
- Medicine kit
- Video camera equipment/tapes
- Roster with starters for announcer

Home Game Procedures

General Checklist

- Mow field.
- Drag infield dirt surface.
- Chalk field.
- Paint bases, pitcher's plate and home plate, including bull pens.
- Set up announcer's area and provide a copy of public address script and inning sponsors.
- Set up scoreboard.
- Set up P.A. system with music.
- Set up concession stand.
- Put up flag.
- Put a gift of seeds, gum, and game ball in opponent dugout.
- Provide both dugouts with water and cups.
- Provide ticket taker with inning promotion sheets and player capsules (refer to Figures 8.2, 8.3, and 8.4).

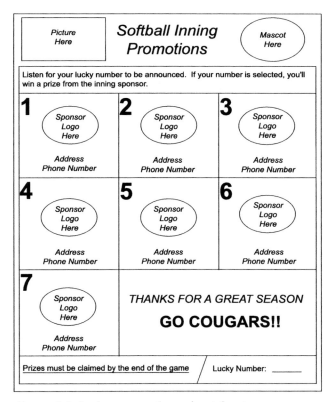

Figure 8.2. Inning promotions sheet front

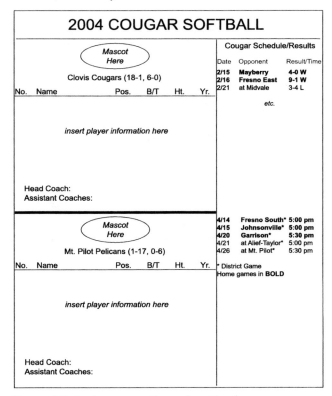

Figure 8.3. Inning promotions sheet back

- Pick up trash on field.
- Blow off bleachers and dugouts.
- Set up ticket taker area.

Inning promotions sheets

Prepare a promotions sheet for the inning sponsors you obtained in November (as described in Chapter 1).

Player capsule

Use the information collected during the initial team meeting in September to make a player capsule sheet as illustrated in Figure 8.4.

Pre-game Warm-Up

- Short team meeting.
- Short jog.
- Stretch.
- Throwing program.
- Whiffle ball soft toss in groups of four (one hitter, one tosser, two shaggers).
- Quick round of pepper – same groups as hitting groups. Player 1 tosses to hitter, she hits in order. If the hitter hits a line drive that is caught, fouls two pitches off, or swings and misses, hitter

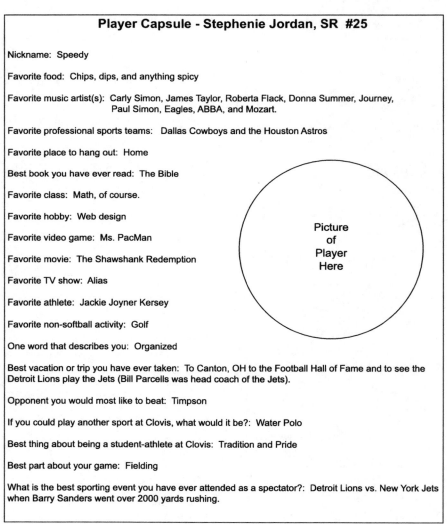

Player Capsule - Stephenie Jordan, SR #25

Nickname: Speedy

Favorite food: Chips, dips, and anything spicy

Favorite music artist(s): Carly Simon, James Taylor, Roberta Flack, Donna Summer, Journey, Paul Simon, Eagles, ABBA, and Mozart.

Favorite professional sports teams: Dallas Cowboys and the Houston Astros

Favorite place to hang out: Home

Best book you have ever read: The Bible

Favorite class: Math, of course.

Favorite hobby: Web design

Favorite video game: Ms. PacMan

Favorite movie: The Shawshank Redemption

Favorite TV show: Alias

Favorite athlete: Jackie Joyner Kersey

Favorite non-softball activity: Golf

One word that describes you: Organized

Best vacation or trip you have ever taken: To Canton, OH to the Football Hall of Fame and to see the Detroit Lions play the Jets (Bill Parcells was head coach of the Jets).

Opponent you would most like to beat: Timpson

If you could play another sport at Clovis, what would it be?: Water Polo

Best thing about being a student-athlete at Clovis: Tradition and Pride

Best part about your game: Fielding

What is the best sporting event you have ever attended as a spectator?: Detroit Lions vs. New York Jets when Barry Sanders went over 2000 yards rushing.

Picture of Player Here

Figure 8.4. Player capsule

goes to the end of the fielding line (far left) and the front of the hitting line becomes the hitter. Players stand 15 feet apart. If a fielder makes an error, she goes to the end of the fielding line.

- Ground balls, fly balls; infielders and outfielders separate. Your pre-game infield/outfield routine should be enough to get the girls warmed up so they feel comfortable and are ready to play. Use the basic pre-game routine described in Chapter 3.

Keeping Stats During the Game

Use your assistant coaches, players on the bench, managers, knowledgeable parents, or boosters to keep stats for you. Consider using the following forms.

Hitting Chart

The hitting chart is fully explained in Chapter 7 and should be used for your opponent's line-up as well as your own team. Refer to Figure 7.2.

Pitching Charts

Chart your pitcher's performance on the form illustrated in Figure 8.5. This chart is a valuable coaching tool and should be reviewed with your pitcher in a one-on-one situation. Also, use Figure 7.3 to record the opponent's pitch tendencies during the game.

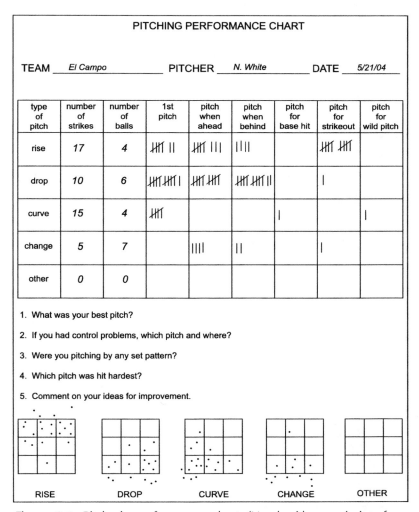

PITCHING PERFORMANCE CHART

TEAM ___El Campo___ PITCHER ___N. White___ DATE ___5/21/04___

type of pitch	number of strikes	number of balls	1st pitch	pitch when ahead	pitch when behind	pitch for base hit	pitch for strikeout	pitch for wild pitch
rise	17	4	⑷⑴ II	⑷⑴ III	IIII		⑷⑴ ⑷⑴	
drop	10	6	⑷⑴⑷⑴ I	⑷⑴ ⑷⑴	⑷⑴ ⑷⑴ II		I	
curve	15	4	⑷⑴			I		I
change	5	7		IIII	II		I	
other	0	0						

1. What was your best pitch?

2. If you had control problems, which pitch and where?

3. Were you pitching by any set pattern?

4. Which pitch was hit hardest?

5. Comment on your ideas for improvement.

RISE   DROP   CURVE   CHANGE   OTHER

Figure 8.5. Pitcher's performance chart (Used with permission from *Baseball/Softball Playbook* by Ron Polk and Donna LoPiano)

Point Chart

The point chart illustrated in Figure 8.6 combines subjective and objective factors, giving you a better indication of performance during a game. Rather than just recording hits and on-base percentage, this chart assigns points for a lack of hustle (-5), sacrifice hits (+3), advancing a runner one base (+1), not scoring a runner at third (-2 points), etc. Points are doubled if a player does anything off the bench.

Production Rating Chart

Batting average doesn't always tell the story of how well a player is hitting, so consider using the production-rating chart illustrated in Figure 8.7. Each batter is awarded points according to the following criteria:

- 0 points – Batter swings and misses for a strikeout, takes a called third strike, or foul tips the ball directly back to the catcher.

- 1 point – Batter swings and pops the ball up in the infield area.

- 2 points – Batter swings and hits a weak fly ball to the outfield.

- 3 points – Batter swings and hits a ground ball to the infield.

- 4 points – Batter swings and hits a deep fly ball, hits a fly ball to advance a runner, or hits a ground ball to advance a runner.

- 5 points – Batter swings and hits a hard ground ball or successfully sacrifice bunts.

POINT CHART

Clovis vs. _____ *Date* _____

DEFENSIVE POINTS

		#4	#12	#2	#7	#11	#34	#3	#15	#28	#25	#13	#14
1st out of an inning	+1												
Double play (all players)	+2												
Pick off (all players)	+2												
No errors w/3 chances	+2												
OF - throws out runner	+3												
C - throws out runner	+3												
C - no passed balls	+2												
Clutch play (dive, etc.)	+4												
Def. play of the game	+5												
Making an error	-1												
Missing a cut off	-3												
Mental error	-4												
Lack of hustle	-5												

OFFENSIVE POINTS

		#4	#12	#2	#7	#11	#34	#3	#15	#28	#25	#13	#14
Lead off hitter on base	+1												
Base hit / walk	+1												
Double	+2												
Triple	+3												
Home Run	+4												
Hit ball with 2 strikes	+1												
Advance runner 1 base	+1												
Sacrifice	+3												
Squeeze	+3												
RBI	+2												
Run scored	+2												
Stolen base	+2												
Game winning hit	+5												
Clutch play	+5												
Not scoring rnr @ 3rd	-2												
Missed SAC or sqz	-2												
Called strike three	-3												
No class	-3												
Mental error	-4												
Lack of hustle	-5												

*POINTS ARE DOUBLED IF DONE OFF THE BENCH

Figure 8.6. Point chart (Used with permission from *Baseball/Softball Playbook* by Ron Polk and Donna LoPiano)

- 6 points – Batter swings and hits a line drive.

To determine the rating, take the total points divided by the number of at-bats. For example, if Claire had three at-bats and hit a line drive on each at bat, she would score 18 points, and her rating would be 6 (18 points divided by 3 = 6).

Scorebook

Use the information in your scorebook and enter the data into a statistics program of your choice. A statistics program is a valuable tool used to generate a complete statistical analysis for your players and team.

Coaching Points

As you watch the game, make an analysis so that in between innings you can make adjustments, if necessary. Don't just watch the movement of the ball, but be aware of the entire field. Remember, you are not a spectator. Try to analyze play by considering the following:

- Your defense: Are your players communicating? Are they adjusting from hitter to hitter? Are they aggressive during bunt situations? How is the ball bouncing on the dirt?

PRODUCTION RATING CHART

RATING	PRODUCTIVITY
0	Batter swings and misses; takes called third strike; foul tips the ball directly back to the catcher.
1	Batter swings and pops the ball up in the infield area.
2	Batter swings and hits a weak fly ball to the outfield.
3	Batter swings and hits a ground ball to the infield.
4	Batter swings and hits a deep fly ball; hits a fly ball to advance a runner; hits a ground ball to advance a runner.
5	Batter swings and hits a hard ground ball; successful sacrifice bunt.
6	Batter swings and hits a line drive.

Hitter	Productivity	At-Bats	Pts.	Rating
Scott, C.	line drive, line drive, line drive	3	18	6
Smith, J.	weak fly to OF, pop-up in IF, called third strike	3	3	1
etc.				

Figure 8.7. Production rating chart (Used with permission from *Baseball/Softball Playbook* by Ron Polk and Donna LoPiano)

- Your offense: Are the players adjusting to the pitcher's pitches? Are they playing as a team by advancing runners? Are they swinging at good pitches?

- Opponent's defense: Do they have a weak link in the field? Does their catcher throw well? Does their outfield throw well? Do they play the bunt situation aggressively?

- Opponent's offense: Who is swinging the bat well? Are they utilizing the bunt and steal? Where is the weak part of their line-up? Are they free swinging?

These are some questions to keep in mind during the entire course of the game so you can make adjustments either between innings or between games. Between innings, be positive and give specific feedback. For example, "Keep your hands back while hitting. The pitcher is throwing a lot of change-ups. Think about hitting the ball to the right side." Also, do not overload your team with too much information; two or three comments or changes are sufficient.

After the Game

Meet with the team in the outfield. Give them feedback and be positive, whether you won or lost.

Get players that need treatment to the training room.

Call in your scores to a local paper, and have the following information ready:

- Your opponent and the final score
- Score by innings
- All stats
- Top performers
- Your current team record
- Who you play next and where

Have managers start rinsing out water bottles and putting equipment away. Be sure a coach stays until all players are gone. Turn out all lights, lock up, and go home.

The Next Day

Enter your statistics into a computer program and post it for your players to see. Write a short newspaper article if you don't have a local sportswriter who covers the games.

Photo: Leslie Scott

9

Season-Ending Responsibilities

May

- Collect equipment
- Work with colleges on recruiting
- Assemble a yearbook
- Prepare for the banquet
- Meet with area coaches to vote on all-district/all-conference selections
- Check athletes' grades
- Mail All-American nomination to NFCA

Collecting Equipment

Collect all equipment and check for damaged items to repair or replace. Compile a list of needs for the next season, with a cost analysis. Order equipment as soon as you can to eliminate the hassle at the beginning of the season (if budgets allow).

Working with Colleges on Recruiting

At the end of the season, send information to colleges on your sophomores and juniors who have the potential or the desire to compete at the collegiate level. If any senior is unsigned or uncommitted, help her! You must remember *you are her agent.*

Video for College Recruiters

❑ Introduction

Have the athlete introduce herself, including her name, number, positions she plays, and color of her jersey.

❑ Individual Skills (with or without teammates)

- Fielding/hitting
- Pitching: highlight her entire repertoire – rise, change, etc.

- Hitting: basic swing mechanics
- Throwing: catchers and outfielders
- Base running: home to first, home to second, home to home

When filming these individual skills, make sure the player and the ball are in the frame. Pull back far enough to show where the ball is coming from and where it lands.

❑ Game Clips

These clips must sell the coach in three minutes or less. Make sure the player's number is clearly visible in the footage.

Be sure to include the athlete's name, number, and school on the label of the video. Include her season statistics, career statistics, or both with the cover letter as well. Make plenty of copies of the tape, and keep the original. College coaches may not send tapes back.

The reality is that Division I college coaches are recruiting players from summer travel teams. Get your kids involved in a travel program if possible. This activity will greatly increase their chances of getting that college scholarship and playing at the Division I level.

Assembling a Yearbook

The yearbook is something that can be as simple or elaborate as you want and can be used in place of a media guide. The following items are examples of what you might include:

Front Cover

Consider using a team picture or a picture of the mascot on the front cover. Color obviously looks the best, but black and white looks fine, too. Refer to Figure 9.1 for an example of a front-cover layout.

Table of Contents

- School information sheet
- Schedule
- Individual statistics
- Game statistics
- Season totals
- Team stats for the season
- A top-5 list
- Newspaper articles
- All-District selections
- Letter to athletes
- Pictures taken throughout the season

❑ School Information Sheet

Include a list of the district opponents, names of important administrators, school address, mascot, and school colors (refer to Figure 9.2).

Anywhere
High School

Team Picture
or
Mascot

2004 Lady Toucans
Varsity Softball

Figure 9.1. Sample front cover layout

Anywhere High School
P.O. Box 12345
Anywhere, TX 70000

School Mascot	Pelican
School Colors	Brown/Black
District	1-5A
Region	III
Superintendent	Skip Noel
Principal	Tony Peterson
Athletic Director	Jody Jordan
Head Coach	Mike Noel

Figure 9.2. School information sheet

❑ Individual Statistics

Include each athlete's picture with a brief description of her season accomplishments (refer to Figure 9.3). The first example is of someone who played, and the second is of someone who didn't.

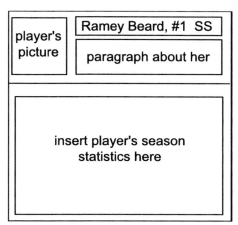

Figure 9.3. Sample individual page

Player #1:

Rebekah was a regular starter for us this season and did an excellent job at second base. She led the team in stolen bases, with 35 during the regular season. The highlight of her season was a game-winning triple to secure a win and a trip to the playoffs. She is also on the Top-5 list for batting average and on-base percentage.

Player #2

Sonya was a back-up first baseman this year and, when called upon, did an outstanding job. Her best performance was at the Mt. Pilot game, where she had a hit and two put-outs. She made other great contributions and will definitely see more action on the field next year.

Top-5 List

Rank players in the following categories; you can add more if you desire (refer to Figure 9.4): runs, RBIs, fielding percentage, hits.

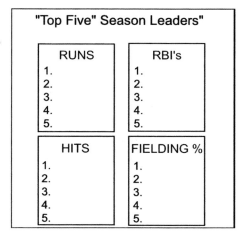

Figure 9.4. Top-5 list

Letter to Athletes

Add a personal note to the back of the yearbook reflecting on the year and encouraging the returning members to work hard for next year. Figure 9.5 illustrates an example of a personal note.

The dedication and hard work exhibited by the 2003 Girls' Varsity Softball Team paid dividends beyond initial expectations. A team that consisted primarily of underclassmen excelled to its maximum potential by season's end. I am extremely proud of this group and look forward to next season.

The opening game against Mayberry wasn't what we had hoped for, but as the season progressed, the skill level and confidence steadily improved. A play-off berth was a great accomplishment for this team and, with the majority of the girls returning, the 2004 season looks very promising. With continued hard work and dedication, our season looks to be a month longer next year!

Work hard this summer and remember, "Winners are ordinary people with extraordinary determination!"

Sincerely,

Coach Jordan

Figure 9.5. Letter to athletes

Preparing for the Banquet

The Awards

Order plaques for special awards well in advance. You may have to do this through the athletic office. The athletic director may just need the names of special award winners such as the most valuable player.

The Speech

Keep one thing in mind: *be brief*. Figure 9.6 illustrates a relatively brief banquet speech.

I'm so honored to have the opportunity to present to you the 2003 Girls' Softball Team. We finished the season with a record of _____ and ended up _____ place in the district.

(Discuss any great wins or playoff experiences here.)

I would now like to present to you several individual awards.

(Include awards such as "Most Improved," "Spirit," "Newcomer of the Year," "Most Valuable Player," etc.)

(To present the MVP award say something like:)

She led the team in hitting, steals, and fielding percentage. She is dedicated to the sport and is an exceptional athlete, leader, and student. The award goes to _____.

Figure 9.6. Sample banquet speech

Meeting with Area Coaches to Vote on All-District/All-Conference Selections

When it is time to meet with your colleagues and decide on All-District selections, you might encounter the following "traditional" meeting format. Major awards should be voted on first (e.g., most valuable player, newcomer of the year, defensive player of the year, offensive player of the year). Players who receive one of the major awards are then eliminated from the rest of the voting to give other athletes an opportunity to be nominated. Coaches are not allowed to vote for their own players.

After the major awards have been given, the coaches should decide how many athletes should be on the first team list (for example, one first baseman, two pitchers, four outfielders). Nominations are then taken for a first baseman. One person at the board should write down all the nominations from each coach with the following information: name, school, position, and classification.

When all the nominations are made, each coach votes for one player for each position. Coaches may not vote for their own athletes. These votes can be made on any type of note paper, including scraps of paper. The results are then tallied on the board. The top vote-getters are the first team selections. In the event of a tie, you may revote to break the tie, or coaches may mutually agree to add the extra player.

The names left on the board that were not selected for first team may be left on the board to be considered for second team selection. Any additional spots can be filled by new nominations and a vote. You can also choose to erase the board and start the nominating process all over. Once the voting is complete, coaches may then add whomever they want to the honorable mention selections without a group vote.

Checking Athletes' Grades

Check each athlete's grades at the end of the year. Many coaches overlook this task when the season is over, but keeping a close eye on grades lets your players know you are serious about their academic success.

Mailing All-American Nomination to NFCA

If you joined the National Fastpitch Coaches Association (NFCA), mail them your nomination for All-American.

June

- Attend youth league and travel team games
- Organize a summer league
- Have a camp

Attending Youth League and Travel Team Games

Encouraging and supporting your youth softball leagues, as well as travel ball, will let the community and potential players know you are interested in them. Spending your personal time watching your current and future players participate on other teams shows them that you care about them beyond the boundaries of your team.

Organizing a Summer League

Starting a summer league program will give your girls valuable game experience, especially if your school is in a rural area and club ball is not an option. To get started, take the following steps:

- Get approval from the administration to use the facilities for games and practices.

- Have your high school girls sign up and pay a fee that should cover insurance, uniforms, and officials.

- Talk with surrounding schools to set up a league schedule.

- Schedule several tournaments to attend during the summer. These tournaments will be an additional cost for the girls, so let them know up front. Entry fees usually run from $100 to $250 per team.

- Consider including younger grades if you have plenty of volunteer coaches.

- Meet with your volunteers to schedule practices. This planning will prevent conflicts when using the facilities.

Having a Camp

Have a camp during the middle of June. Ask former players who play in college to help and split the profits with them.

Photo: David Menedian

10

Off-Season Training

Planning

Reflect on the season, look over your practice sheets, watch game film, study your season statistics, and then decide what your team's weaknesses were and how you can improve them. It might be conditioning, hitting, defensive strategy, or strength. Whatever it is, concentrate on that weakness during the off-season. The off-season is also a good time to reinforce basic fundamentals, but specific emphasis should be placed on getting faster and stronger during this time. Use the season to improve in the game of softball.

Off-Season Activities

The off-season should be geared to a basic enhancement of physical fitness, including improvement in speed, agility, and strength. Divide your off-season into three phases: general, intermediate, and concentrated (or phase one, phase two, and phase three). Among the types of activities that should be included in your off-season program are the following:

Speed Drills

A2's—This drill is similar to a skipping motion, but with emphasis on good sprint mechanics. Instead of skipping with a straight leg, the thigh comes up parallel with the ground. The foot should also be parallel to the ground rather than hanging down as if pointing the toe. Emphasis should be placed on getting as many contacts on the ground in the required distance.

B2's—Also known as a pawing drill, the mechanics are similar to the A2. After driving the knee, the foot should kick out so the leg is extended and parallel to the ground. At this point, the foot should be pulled down to the ground in a pawing action, striking the ground under the body.

Heel ups—This exercise is similar to what we all know as butt kicks. The heels just need to come high under the body in a quick cycle. Again, emphasize quickness and making contact with the ground as many times as possible in a short distance.

Plyometrics

Double-leg bound—Jump outward and upward using forward thrusting movements of the arms with no pause between jumps.

Alternate-leg bound—This exercise involves an exaggerated running motion. Start the athletes at a jog and gradually get them to drive the knees up toward the chest. The idea is to gain as much height and distance as possible.

Single-leg bound—Hop with one leg at a time, also trying to gain as much height and distance as possible.

Squat jump—Jump up and down continuously, using a full squatting motion when on the ground.

Tuck jump—This jump is also up and down, but the emphasis is on bringing the knees to the chest at the height of the jump.

Scissor jump—Start in a lunge position, and jump as high and straight in the air as possible, using the arms to gain lift. At the top of the jump, the legs are reversed before landing.

Jump Rope Routines

Make sure the jump rope is the appropriate length for each athlete. Measure from the tops of the athlete's feet to her armpit. Work each of the following exercises for 30 seconds.

- Both feet single jumps
- Right foot single jumps
- Left foot single jumps
- Both feet side to side over a line
- Both feet front and back over a line
- Two jumps left foot, two jumps right foot, single jumps
- Right foot side to side over a line
- Left foot side to side over a line
- Right foot front and back over a line
- Left foot front and back over a line
- Both feet three single jumps, one double jump
- Both feet consecutive double jumps

Medicine Ball Drills

Squat throw—Bend down in a squatting position with the medicine ball between the legs. Explode upward, throwing the ball in the air. Upon catching it, squat immediately and repeat the sequence.

Trunk twist—Two athletes stand back-to-back with one medicine ball. As athlete #1 turns to the right to pass the ball, athlete #2 turns left to receive it. Athlete #2 then quickly turns to pass to her right while athlete #1 receives the ball from her left. Rotate after 10 to 20 reps.

Sit-up throw—Two athletes sit on the floor, facing each other with feet locked. Athlete #1 holds the ball above her head, while athlete #2 is sitting, waiting to receive the ball. Athlete #1 lies backward, comes up, and throws to athlete #2. Athlete #2 receives the ball and bends backward to absorb the shock of the throw, thereby engaging the abdominal muscles. As athlete #2 comes forward, she throws to athlete #1, who also receives the ball, bends backward, and absorbs the shock. The pattern continues for 10 to 20 reps.

Chest pass—Two athletes should be on their knees, about six to eight feet apart, facing each other. The ball is pushed rapidly by one athlete to the other, with each girl extending her arms completely.

Overhead pass—Two athletes should stand 10 to 12 feet apart and, using an overhead passing motion, pass the ball back and forth to each other.

Weight Training

Start your weight-training program by maxing out on your core lifts: bench, squat, dead lift, and hang cleans. This activity will give you an idea of who should be grouped together. Put three athletes in each group, so that one athlete is lifting, one is spotting, and one is working on a supplemental lift.

Each group will rotate through the core lift and wait for other groups to finish.

Demand precision and discipline in the weight room so no one gets injured. Have the athletes stand at their current station until everyone is finished. When everyone is standing, break it down and move to the next station, keeping everyone on the same pace. Figure 10.1 shows an example of a weight room layout.

The following stations, with the core lift noted first, are recommended:

- *Squat*, calf raises
- Alternate these exercises:
  - ❏ *Bench*, incline flyes
  - ❏ *Incline*, flat-bench flyes
- *Dead lift*, crunches
- *Hang cleans*, hamstring curls, leg extensions (since a spotter isn't necessary, have two supplemental lifts)

- *Hip flexibility* (each group of three steps over and under five hurdles until everyone else is finished)

Agility Activities

All running and conditioning should be done outside, but in case of bad weather, consider doing the following activities in a gym.

Conditioning Circuit

Station 1 – Crunches

Station 2 – Push-ups

Station 3 – Jump rope

Station 4 – Step-ups

Station 5 – Jogging

Station 6 – Speed weights or medicine ball drills

Cone Drills

On all jumps, weight should be over the toes, shoulders forward, eyes level, and contact on the

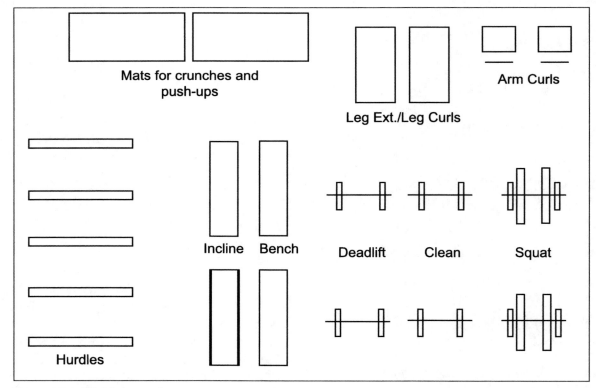

Figure 10.1. Weight room layout

ground should be quick. Do each drill from both sides, and then repeat two to three times.

- Three foot contacts side to side, then sprint forward five yards (see Figure 10.2).

- Three foot contacts front to back, then sprint five yards.

- Three foot contacts side to side, then three slide shuffle steps.

- Eight foot contacts (see Figure 10.3).

- Twelve foot contacts (see Figure 10.4).

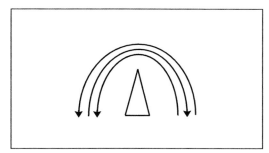

Figure 10.2. Three foot contacts

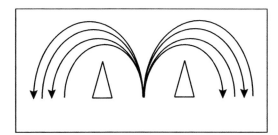

Figure 10.3. Eight foot contacts

Figure 10.4. Twelve foot contacts

Cone Jumps

Use eight cones in a straight line, approximately 18 to 24 inches apart.

- One-cone jump: Face forward, feet together, get off the ground quickly, and stick the last jump over the cones (see Figure 10.5).

- Two-cone jump: Face forward, feet together, get off the ground quickly, jump over two cones instead of one, and stick the last jump over the cones (see Figure 10.6).

- Zigzag: Feet together, jump forward at an angle over the cones (see Figure 10.7).

- Two-step shuffle: Facing sideways, step with each foot between the cones as quickly as possible.

- Lateral jumps: Same as the two-step shuffle, except land with feet together between the cones.

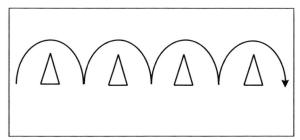

Figure 10.5. One-cone jump

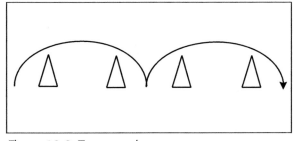

Figure 10.6. Two-cone jump

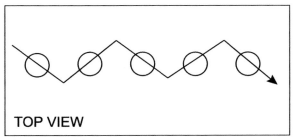

Figure 10.7. Zigzag

Square Drills

The cones should be 10 to 15 feet apart. Players should keep their weight over their toes, hips low, and do each drill going both directions (see Figure 10.8).

- sprint-shuffle-backpedal
- shuffle-backpedal-shuffle
- backpedal-shuffle-sprint

- shuffle-sprint-shuffle
- backpedal-sprint-backpedal
- shuffle-shuffle-shuffle-sprint-shuffle-shuffle-shuffle
- sprint-backpedal-sprint-shuffle-backpedal-sprint-backpedal
- backpedal-sprint-backpedal-shuffle-backpedal-sprint-backpedal

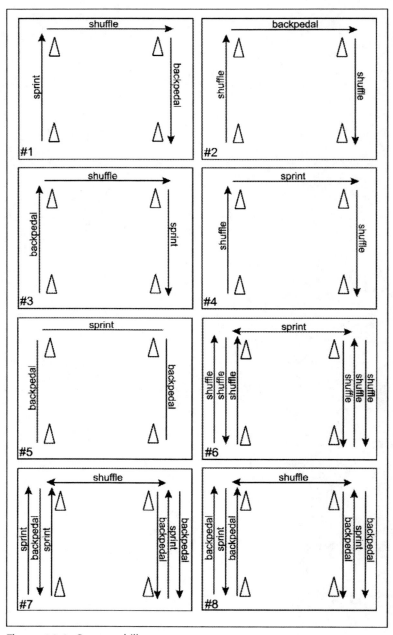

Figure 10.8. Square drills

Conditioning

Pacers—Start at half-court on a basketball court. Sprint to the baseline, turn around, and sprint back to the free-throw line, then back to the baseline, to the top of the key, and back to the baseline. Sprint the entire length of the floor to the opposite baseline, and repeat the same thing on that half of the court. Finish by sprinting back through the half-court line (see Figure 10.9). This routine should take 30 seconds to finish, with an additional one minute and 30 seconds for recovery.

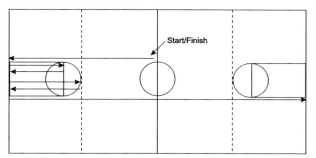

Figure 10.9. Pacers

Disneylands—Start on the side of a football field at the goal line and sprint across the width of the field. At the other end, jog up to the five-yard line, turn, and jog the width of the field again. Jog to the 10-yard line, turn, and walk the width of the field. Continue this pattern (sprint/jog/walk) for the entire length of the field (see Figure 10.10). Take two minutes' rest between each full Disneyland.

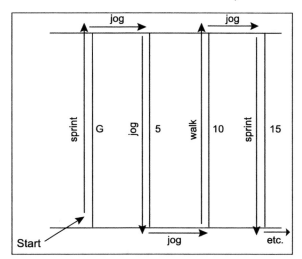

Figure 10.10. Disneylands

50s – Sprint from the goal line on a football field to the 50-yard line. Recovery time should be three times as long as the time it takes you to finish. For example, for a five-second sprint, take 15 seconds of rest.

100s—Sprint from goal line to goal line on a football field. This sprint should take 15 to 17 seconds to finish, with another 45 seconds for recovery.

240s—Sprint from the back of one end zone to the back of the other end zone and back. Walk 120 yards for recovery.

350s—Sprint around the entire football field (end zone included). This sprint should take 70 to 75 seconds to finish. Walk out to the 50-yard line and back to recover.

Gassers—Sprint four times across the width of a football field. It should take 35 to 40 seconds to finish. Walk back across the width of the field to recover.

10-minute drill—Run 10 x 100-yard strides in 10 minutes. For example, if you stride 100 yards in 16 seconds, you have 44 seconds to get back to the starting line and begin another 100-yard stride. The only recovery time is jogging back to start over.

Competition-Day Activities

Another off-season activity that can be used to develop your players involves having your athletes compete against each other in a series of games and drills. To make competition days more interesting, have the assistant coaches pick teams. Drafting players is recommended to ensure a fair distribution of talent. Have coaches draw for first, second, third pick, etc., and pick according to the number of teams and coaches you have. Chart 10.1 illustrates the drafting order for four teams.

Keep a running total of scores until the end of the year to crown a winning team. Assign point totals for first, second, third, and fourth place (10, eight, five, and three points). Choose games (e.g. kick ball) and relays that are not only competitive but athletically challenging as well. The following relays and games are for teams of eight players.

	Rd 1	Rd 2	Rd 3	Rd 4	Rd 5
Tm#1	first pick	fourth pick	third pick	second pick	(start over)
Tm#2	second pick	first pick	fourth pick	third pick	
Tm#3	third pick	second pick	first pick	fourth pick	
Tm#4	fourth pick	third pick	second pick	first pick	

Chart 10.1. Drafting order example

Relays

❑ Relay #1

Set-up: Run this relay on a track. Athletes are stationed at locations on the track, as illustrated in Figure 10.11.

Directions: Team members can decide who will run the following distances: 400m, 200m, 100m, 100m, repeat. Use a relay baton (or something more cumbersome to add a measure of fun/entertainment to the relay).

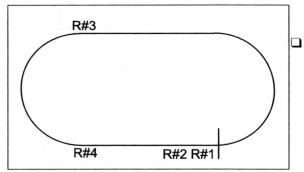

Figure 10.11. Track relay

Relay #2

Set-up: Run this relay on a football field.

Directions: Team members must determine who will do the following:

- Run 50 yards
- Wheelbarrow for 50 yards
- Switch and continue for another 50 yards
- Crab walk for 50 yards
- Bear crawl 50 yards
- Piggyback 50 yards
- Switch and continue for another 50 yards
- Run 50 yards

❑ Relay #3

Set-up: You'll need 10 cones, 10 hurdles, 12 tires, two soccer balls, and plastic for an optional water slide. The set-up for the relay is illustrated in Figure 10.12.

Directions: Run two teams at once and time them. Instead of using a relay baton, just have athletes slap hands.

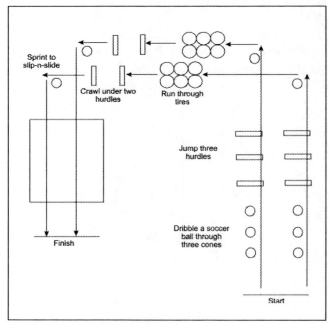

Figure 10.12. Relay #3 – obstacle course

Games

❏ Ultimate Football

Set-up: This game is played on the football field using the width and not the entire length. Use cones and the end zone as boundaries.

Directions: The ball may only be advanced by throwing or pitching it. An athlete may not run forward with the ball, only sideways and backwards. If the ball hits the ground, the ball immediately goes to the other team. Play does not stop unless a touchdown is scored. A team scores by catching the ball in the end zone. If the ball is dropped, no points are scored, and possession reverts to the other team. Play for four quarters or two halves.

Setting Individual Goals

General Goals

Since you have evaluated your team as a whole at the end of the season, your players should also spend time evaluating themselves. The coach and individual player should each fill out a form evaluating the player, and then compare forms. Figure 10.13 shows a sample form to use.

PLAYER EVALUATION SHEET

1. What are your strengths as a softball player?

2. What do you need to work on to reach your potential?

3. What is your plan to improve in these areas?

4. What is your two-strike plan?

5. What are your individual goals for the off-season?

Figure 10.13. Sample player evaluation form

Physical Goals

Have athletes decide on how much they will increase their strength maxes, vertical jump, speed, etc., during the course of the off-season, and keep a record of their goals, as well as their test-evaluation performances, on their workout sheet. Test each athlete in the following areas:

- Strength—squat, hang clean, dead lift, bench press, dips, pull-ups

- Speed—40-yard run

- Quickness and agility—Use one of the square drills illustrated in Figure 10.9.

- Vertical jump

- 800-meter run (tested on a track)

Off-Season Scoring Charts

Use the charts in Tables 10.1 to 10.9 to award point values. Instead of giving points for first, second, third, etc., assign points based on performance. This system allows your athletes to compete against themselves rather than someone else's best performance (as in the tryout evaluation). Consider it the off-season decathlon. Keep records in each event and total points for posterity.

A Sample Off-Season Conditioning Program

Although weight lifting is essential for a well-rounded off-season, it may be difficult to schedule the weight room at a time that works well for everyone on your team. Try to emphasize gaining strength during the summer by sending a summer program home with each of your athletes and opening the weight room for their use. The following conditioning program can be used in the months preceding the season. A summer workout program is included later in this chapter.

❑ Squats

Weight	Pts.	Weight	Pts.	Weight	Pts.
300	1000	245	816	190	633
295	982	240	799	185	616
290	966	235	783	180	599
285	949	230	766	175	583
280	932	225	749	170	566
275	916	220	733	165	549
270	899	215	716	160	533
265	882	210	699	155	516
260	866	205	683	150	499
255	849	200	667	145	483
250	833	195	649	140	466

Table 10.1. Point values for the squat. Note: multiply the amount of weight lifted by 3.3, if that weight is not on the chart.

❑ Bench press

Weight	Pts.	Weight	Pts.	Weight	Pts.
160	1000	125	781	90	563
155	969	120	750	85	531
150	938	115	719	80	500
145	906	110	688	75	469
140	875	105	656	70	438
135	844	100	625	65	406
130	813	95	594	60	375

Table 10.2. Point values for the bench press. Note: Multiply the amount of weight lifted by 6.25, if that weight is not on the chart.

❏ Hang clean

Weight	Pts.	Weight	Pts.	Weight	Pts.
200	1000	155	775	110	550
195	975	150	750	105	525
190	950	145	725	100	500
185	925	140	700	95	475
180	900	135	675	90	450
175	875	130	650	85	425
170	850	125	625	80	400
165	825	120	600	75	375
160	800	115	575	70	350

Table 10.3. Point values for the hang clean. Note: Multiply the weight lifted by 5.0, if that weight it not on the chart.

❏ Dead lift

Weight	Pts.	Weight	Pts.	Weight	Pts.
250	1000	205	820	160	640
245	980	200	800	155	620
240	960	195	780	150	600
235	940	190	760	145	580
230	920	185	740	140	560
225	900	180	720	135	540
220	880	175	700	130	520
215	860	170	680	125	500
210	840	165	660	120	480

Table 10.4. Point values for the dead lift. Note: Multiply the weight lifted by 4.0 if that weight is not on the chart.

❏ Dips

No.	Pts.	No.	Pts.	No.	Pts.
15	1000	10	667	5	334
14	934	9	600	4	267
13	867	8	534	3	200
12	800	7	467	2	133
11	734	6	400	1	67

Table 10.5. Point values for dips. Note: Multiply the amount of dips performed by 66.7, if that number is not on the chart.

❏ Pull-ups

No.	Pts.	No.	Pts.	No.	Pts.
15	1000	10	667	5	334
14	934	9	600	4	267
13	867	8	534	3	200
12	800	7	467	2	133
11	734	6	400	1	67

Table 10.6. Point values for pull-ups. Note: Multiply the number of pull-ups performed by 66.7, if that number is not on the chart.

❏ 40-yard sprint

Time	Pts.	Time	Pts.	Time	Pts.
4.2	1000	4.9	720	5.6	440
4.3	960	5.0	680	5.7	400
4.4	920	5.1	640	5.8	360
4.5	880	5.2	600	5.9	320
4.6	840	5.3	560	6.0	280
4.7	800	5.4	520	6.1	240
4.8	760	5.5	480	6.2	200

Table 10.7. Point values for the 40-yard sprint. Note: Add or subtract 40 points (depending on the time achieved), if that time is not on the chart.

❏ Vertical jump

Inches	Pts.	Inches	Pts.	Inches	Pts.
33	1000	26	788	19	576
32	970	25	757	18	545
31	939	24	727	17	515
30	909	23	697	16	485
29	879	22	667	15	454
28	848	21	636	14	424
27	818	20	606	13	394

Table 10.8. Point values for the vertical jump. Note: Multiply the number of inches by 30.3, if that number is not on the chart.

❏ **800m run**

Time	Pts.	Time	Pts.	Time	Pts.	Time	Pts.
2:45	1000	3:00	850	3:15	700	3:30	550
2:46	990	3:01	840	3:16	690	3:31	540
2:47	980	3:02	830	3:17	680	3:32	530
2:48	970	3:03	820	3:18	670	3:33	520
2:49	960	3:04	810	3:19	660	3:34	510
2:50	950	3:05	800	3:20	650	3:35	500
2:51	940	3:06	790	3:21	640	3:36	490
2:52	930	3:07	780	3:22	630	3:37	480
2:53	920	3:08	770	3:23	620	3:38	470
2:54	910	3:09	760	3:24	610	3:39	460
2:55	900	3:10	750	3:25	600	3:40	450
2:56	890	3:11	740	3:26	590	3:41	440
2:57	880	3:12	730	3:27	580	3:42	430
2:58	870	3:13	720	3:28	570	3:43	420
2:59	860	3:14	710	3:29	560	3:44	410

Table 10.9. Point values for the 800M run. Note: Add or subtract 10 points (depending on the time achieved), if that time is not on the chart.

Phase One (September-October)

Develop a good conditioning base during this phase by focusing on slower, longer runs with less rest between sets. Spend at least one day on the field during this phase to work on fundamentals. Add field days in subsequent phases. Use circuits to focus on one skill or to incorporate several skills in the activity simultaneously.

Sample Week

Monday

- Warm-up
- Disneylands x 3
- Weights: 3 x 10 @ 50% of max on core lifts; 3 x 12 on supplemental lifts

Tuesday

- Softball day (fundamentals)

Wednesday

- Warm-up
- 10-minute drill
- Weights: 3 x 8 @ 65% of max; 3 x 12 on supplemental lifts

Thursday

- Warm-up
- Speed drills: 3 x 30m
- Plyometrics: 3 x 30m or 3 x 10 for stationary jumps

117

Friday

- Warm-up

- 3 x 350s, 3 x 100s, 3 x 50s

- Weights: 3 x 10 @ 50% of max; 3 x 12 on supplemental lifts

Phase Two (November)

Test strength maxes, times, jumps, etc., to assess the athlete's progress before beginning this phase.

Sample Week

Monday

- Warm-up

- 6 x 240s

- Weights: 3 x 8 @ 70%; 3 x 12 on supplemental lifts

Tuesday

- Softball day

Wednesday

- Warm-up

- 3 x gassers, 8 x 100s, 4 x 50s

- Plyometrics: 3 x 30m or 3 x 10 for stationary jumps

- Weights: 3 x 8 @ 70%; 3 x 12 on supplemental lifts

Thursday

- Softball day

Friday

- Warm-up

- Cone drills x 1

- Cone jumps x 2

- Weights: 3 x 8 @ 70%; 3 x 12 on supplemental lifts

Phase Three (December)

Stay with two days a week on the field, but add one day of competition, and don't forget to test maxes one more time.

Sample Week

Monday

- Warm-up

- Pacers x 3

- Weights: 3 x 8 @ 70%; 3 x 12 on supplemental lifts

Tuesday

- Softball day

Wednesday

- Warm-up

- Square drills x 1

- Jump rope routine x 2

- Weights: 3 x 8 @ 70%; 3 x 12 on supplemental lifts

Thursday

- Softball day

Friday

- Competition day

Summer Workout

You can spend a great deal of time building strength, stamina, speed, and agility, but unless your athletes are committed to a summer program, it's all lost. Before school lets out, give your athletes a workout manual and a weight room schedule. Also, encourage all your players to play on a travel team during the summer. Not only will they gain valuable game experience, but summer is also the time when college coaches scout players to recruit.

Sample Summer Workout Manual

Introduction

The following workout program is designed to help each player maintain the conditioning, speed, and strength she worked hard to improve during the off-season. The workout will start the first week in June and will continue until the first week of school begins (about an 11-week period).

The entire program will consist of strength training, circuit training, and a running workout. Each part of the program is fully explained in this manual, and at the end of the manual players will find a training log divided into weeks with sets, reps, times, distances, etc. for team members to follow.

Weight Program

The weight program is based on each player's final max of the year. For core lifts, each team member will be working five sets starting with 10 reps, then 8, 6, 4, and 2 reps. The amount of weight to lift for each set can be determined by the following simple steps: Using the max weight, take 50% to get the 10-rep poundage. Take 60% of the max weight to get the 8-rep poundage, and so on. For example:

Squat max = 220 lbs.
1st set: 220 x .5 = 110 lbs x 10 reps
2nd set: 220 x .6 = 130 lbs x 8 reps
3rd set: 220 x .7 = 155 lbs x 6 reps
4th set: 220 x .8 = 175 lbs x 4 reps
5th set: 220 x .9 = 200 lbs x 2 reps

Two-Week Sample for Squat

❏ Week #1

Monday:	Thursday:
10 x 110 lbs	10 x 110 lbs
8 x 130 lbs	8 x 130 lbs
6 x 155 lbs	6 x 155 lbs
4 x 175 lbs	4 x 175 lbs
2 x 200 lbs	2 x 200 lbs

❏ Week #2

Monday:	Thursday:
10 x 120 lbs	10 x 120 lbs
8 x 140 lbs	8 x 140 lbs
6 x 160 lbs	6 x 160 lbs
4 x 180 lbs	4 x 180 lbs
2 x 205 lbs	2 x 205 lbs

Spacing Workouts

Each player can do upper body one day and lower body the next, or combine all lifts in one day. Always make sure the core lifts (noted in italics in the following examples) are completed. Supplemental lifts can be done as time allows. The following examples illustrate two routines that can be performed over the course of a weeklong period.

❏ Four-day split

Mon: *Bench*, military press, arm curls, upright rows, close-grip bench, push-ups, crunches

Tue: *Squat, hang clean*, stiff-legged dead lift, leg curls, leg extensions, calf raises, step-ups, lunges

Wed: Rest

Thu: *Incline*, military press, arm curls, upright rows, close grip bench, push-ups, crunches

Fri: *Squat, snatch or dead lift*, stiff-legged dead lift, leg curls, leg extensions, calf raises, step-ups, lunges

❏ Two-day split

Mon: *Bench, squat, hang clean*, military press, arm curls, upright rows, close-grip bench, push-ups, crunches, leg curls, leg extensions, calf raises

Thu: *Incline, squat, snatch or dead lift*, military press, arm curls, upright rows, close-grip bench, push-ups, crunches, leg curls, leg extensions, calf raises

Circuit Programs

Weight Circuit

If a team member is unable to get to a weight room, she can use the following circuit.

- Wall sits—Legs at 90-degree angles, back flat, and hands at sides for 45 seconds at a time.

- Chair dip—Using two chairs, put feet on one and palms on the other with arms behind the back. Lower the body toward the floor with arms at 90 degrees, then push back up. Repeat for three sets of 10.

- Push-ups—Regular straight leg push-ups (3 x 10).

- Toe raises—Balance with one hand against the wall and raise one heel at a time for three sets of 25 (each leg).

- Lunges—Do three sets of about 30 yards each.

Jump Rope Circuit

Start out doing each station for 30 seconds, and increase to one minute by summer's end.

- Both feet single jumps

- Right foot single jumps

- Left foot single jumps

- Both feet side to side over a line

- Both feet front and back over a line

- Two jumps left foot—two jumps right foot—single jumps

- Right foot side to side over a line

- Left foot side to side over a line

- Right foot front and back over a line

- Left foot front and back over a line

- Both feet three single jumps—one double jump

- Both feet consecutive double jumps

Abdominal Circuit

- Slide ups—Lie on back with arms rested on thighs (palms down). Raise back and shoulders off the ground and slide hands to knees. When hands touch knees, slowly slide back (3 x 20).

- Obliques—Lie on back with arms behind head. Have a partner hold onto your arms. Lift both legs so the bottoms of the feet are pointing to the ceiling. Lower legs to the right so the right leg touches the ground, then go left. Keep both feet together (3 x 10).

- Crunches—Lie on back with knees bent and hands over chest. Raise shoulders off the floor and then go back down. For a variation, rest legs on a bench or lift them off the floor (3 x 25).

- Reverse sit-ups—Lie on back with legs in the air so that the bottoms of the feet are pointing at the ceiling. Slowly raise the pelvis and lower the back off the floor and then go back down in a controlled manner. Do not rock; use only the pelvis muscles (3 x 10).

- V-sits—Lie on back with arms over the head and legs straight. At the same time, bring arms up and legs up and try to touch the feet above the center of the body. Lower arms and legs slowly (3 x 10).

Plyometric Circuit

Do this circuit on grass and work each exercise 3 x 30 yards.

- Double leg bound—Jump outward and upward, using forward thrusting movements of the arms with no pause between jumps.

- Alternate leg bound—Use an exaggerated running motion. Start at a jog and gradually drive the knees up toward the chest. The idea is to gain as much height and distance as possible.

- Single leg bound—Hop with one leg at a time, also trying to gain as much height and distance as possible.

• Squat jump—Jump up and down, using a full squatting motion when on the ground. This jump should be continuous.

• Tuck jump—This jump is also up and down, but emphasis is on bringing the knees to the chest at the height of the jump.

• Scissor jump—Start in a lunge position and jump as high and straight in the air as possible, using the arms to gain lift. At the top of the jump, the legs are reversed before landing.

Bleacher Circuit

Make sure to watch out on the way up and down. Sprint up the stairs but walk slowly as you come down to ensure good footing and to take stress off the knees.

• Version #1—Sprint to the top, one step at a time, and walk down slowly. Do this for 10 minutes of continuous running, using the walk down as the recovery.

• Version #2—If running at a football stadium, start at the far left, sprint up, and walk back down the same way. Jog to the middle of the bleachers, sprint up, walk down the same way. Jog to the far right, sprint up, walk down, and then jog down out of the bleachers (or walk down the steps). Jog under the bleachers to the starting point at the far left. Repeat this pattern five times; increase to 10 reps by the end of the summer.

Aquatic Circuit

Part one—waist-deep water

• Jog two minutes

• Tuck jumps 10 times

• High knees

• Skipping

• Frog jumps 10 times

• Backwards jog

Part two—shoulder-deep water

• Back to wall—arms extended, holding on to side—kick for one minute, but do not break the water

• Back to wall—arms extended, holding on to side—kick for one minute, breaking the water

• Face wall—hold on to side—kick for one minute, but do not break the water

• Face wall—hold on to side—kick for one minute, breaking the water

Part three—deep water

• Tread water, using legs only, keeping hands out of water—five minutes

• Tread water, using arms only—five minutes

Part four—shoulder-deep water

• Arms extended out to side—pull arms down to legs 10 times

• Arms at legs—pull up out of water 10 times

• Arms extended out in front—pull down to side of body 10 times

• Arms at side of body—pull up out of water 10 times

• Hold on to side for balance, start with legs together—pull one leg up in front 10 times

• Start leg extended in front of body—pull down 10 times (work both legs)

Running/Agility Workout

Each of the following have been fully explained earlier in this chapter:

• Cone drills

• Cone jumps

• Square drills

• Line drills

• Conditioning: Pacers, Disneylands, 50s, 100s, etc.

Training Log

Mark only those items completed. Players may also choose to lift two days a week.

Week One

Tuesday, May 26th:
- ___ 30-minute cardio (jog or bike)
- ___ Weights (10, 8, 6, 4, 2)

Thursday, May 28th:
- ___ 30-minute cardio

Friday, May 29th:
- ___ 30-minute cardio
- ___ Weights (10, 8, 6, 4, 2)

Week Two

Tuesday, June 2nd:
- ___ 30-minute cardio
- ___ Weights (10, 8, 6, 4, 2)

Thursday, June 4th:
- ___ Square drills x 1
- ___ Cone jumps x 1
- ___ 30-minute cardio

Friday, June 5th:
- ___ Weights (10, 8, 6, 4, 2)

Week Three

Tuesday, June 9th:
- ___ Speed drills x 1
- ___ 350s x 5
- ___ Weights (10, 8, 6, 4, 2)

Thursday, June 11th:
- ___ Disneylands x 3

Friday, June 12th:
- ___ Speed drills x 1
- ___ 350s x 5
- ___ Weights (10, 8, 6, 4, 2)

Week Four

Tuesday, June 16th:
- ___ Square drills x 2
- ___ 350s x 4
- ___ Weights (10, 8, 6, 4, 2)

Thursday, June 18th:
- ___ Disneylands x 3

Friday, June 19th:
- ___ Square drills x 2
- ___ 350s x 4
- ___ Weights (10, 8, 6, 4, 2)

Week Five

Tuesday, June 23rd:
- ___ Square drills x 1
- ___ Cone jumps x 1
- ___ Weights (3 x 10)
- ___ Plyometrics 3 x 10

Thursday, June 25th:
- ___ Pacers x 3

Friday, June 26th:
- ___ Gassers x 3
- ___ 100s x 8
- ___ 50s x 4
- ___ Weights (3 x 10)

Week Six

Tuesday, June 30th:
- ____ Square drills x 1
- ____ Cone jumps x 2
- ____ Bleachers (Version 1)
- ____ Pacers x 3
- ____ Aquatic circuit x 1

Thursday, July 2nd:
- ____ Max out
- Bench: ____ Squat: ____ Hang clean: ____
- Dead lift: ____

Friday, July 3rd: No Workout – Enjoy the 4th!

Week Seven

Tuesday, July 7th:
- ____ Square drills x 2
- ____ Bleachers (Version 1)
- ____ Pacers x 3
- ____ Weights (10, 8, 6, 4, 2)

Thursday, July 9th:
- ____ Cone drills x 2
- ____ Abdominals 3 x 10
- ____ Aquatic circuit x 1

Friday, July 10th:
- ____ Plyometrics x 2
- ____ 350s x 3
- ____ 240s x 2
- ____ 50s x 4

Week Eight

Tuesday, July 14th:
- ____ Cone jumps x 2
- ____ Abdominals 3 x 10
- ____ Square drills x 1
- ____ Pacers x 5
- ____ Weights (10, 8, 6, 4, 2)

Thursday, July 16th:
- ____ Cone drills x 2
- ____ Abdominals 3 x 10
- ____ Aquatic circuit x 1
- ____ Plyometrics 3 x 10

Friday, July 17th:
- ____ Gassers x 3
- ____ 100s x 4
- ____ 50s x 4
- ____ Weights (10, 8, 6, 4, 2)

Week Nine

Tuesday, July 21st:
- ____ Cone drills x 2
- ____ Square drills x 2
- ____ Pacers x 5
- ____ Weights (10, 8, 6, 4, 2)

Thursday, July 23rd:
- ____ Plyometrics 3 x 10
- ____ Abdominals 3 x 10
- ____ Pacers x 3
- ____ Aquatic circuit x 1

Friday, July 24th:
- ____ Gassers x 4
- ____ 100s x 8
- ____ Weights (10, 8, 6, 4, 2)

Week Ten

Tuesday, July 28th:
- ___ Cone drills x 2
- ___ Square drills x 2
- ___ Pacers x 5
- ___ Weights (10, 8, 6, 4, 2)

Thursday, July 30th:
- ___ Bleachers (Version 2)
- ___ Abdominals 3 x 10
- ___ Pacers x 3
- ___ Aquatic circuit x 1

Friday, July 31st:
- ___ 350s x 3
- ___ Gassers x 3
- ___ 50s x 5
- ___ Weights (10, 8, 6, 4, 2)

Week Eleven

Tuesday, August 4th:
- ___ 350s x 3
- ___ Gassers x 3
- ___ 50s x 5
- ___ Weights (3 x 10)

Thursday, August 6th:
- ___ Plyometrics 3 x 10
- ___ Abdominals 3 x 10
- ___ Pacers x 3

Friday, August 7th:
- ___ Disneylands x 3
- ___ Weights (3 x 10)

A

Planning a Tournament

Three to Four Months Before the Tournament

Send a letter to prospective teams. If your tournament is yearly, then you will probably already have a few teams that are regulars. For your open spots, get the coaching directory out and start addressing letters. Some schools may have already committed to a tournament at the end of last year's season, but it doesn't hurt to try to recruit them for the next year. Figure A.1 shows an example of a letter to send. You might want to include a self-addressed stamped envelope for the response cards. Figure A.2 shows an example of a response card.

Six Weeks Before the Tournament

Send another letter confirming participation in the tournament, with a list of the teams entered, an information sheet for the program, a bracket, and a

---

2004 Easter Softball Classic

September 2, 2003

Dear Coach/Athletic Director:

The 2004 season will be approaching and we would like to invite you to participate in our annual Easter Classic. As in the past, Clovis High School and Katy High School will be hosting the Easter Softball Classic on April 3rd, 5th, and 6th, 2004. The 2003 Classic was very successful and, with the input we received last year, we plan on making this year's tournament even better. Once again, we will make every effort to give each team as many games as possible.

The tournament format will be pool play followed by playoffs and your junior varsity team is also invited to compete. There will be two varsity divisions: The Small School (under 1200 enrollment) and the Large School (over 1200 enrollment). If you wish to play up in the large school division, you may.

The entry fees are as follows: $325 for varsity only, $225 for junior varsity only, and $550 for both varsity and junior varsity. Entries will be taken in the order they are received. We can only accommodate a certain number of teams, so you must respond in a timely fashion to secure a spot for your team. Send your entry fee to Mike Noel, Clovis High School, 1234 Anywhere Street, Clovis, CA 99876. Make checks payable to Easter Softball Classic.

Important Note: If your school's spring break does not fall during the week of the tournament, we will make every effort to schedule the majority of your games after 2:00 pm. Please note this on the return letter.

Please send in your response sheet as soon as possible, so we can set up the tournament without delay. We look forward to hearing from you. Additional information will be sent after we have your response. If you have any questions or need additional information, please do not hesitate to contact the tournament directors:

Mike Noel
CHS: (559) 555-1212
Home: (559) 555-1213

Stephenie Jordan
KHS: (832) 555-1212
Home: (832) 555-1214

We hope to hear from you soon.

Mike Noel, Clovis Softball

Figure A.1. Sample letter to teams

```
2004 EASTER SOFTBALL CLASSIC
April 3rd, 5th, and 6th

Entry Fees:
$325 (Varsity)
$225 (JV)
$550 (Varsity & JV)

Make checks payable to:
Easter Softball Classic

Mail to:
Mike Noel
1111 Anywhere Street
Clovis, CA  98765

School Name: _____     Phone #: _____

Coach's Name: _____     Home #: _____

(  ) Yes, we will participate.

(  ) No, we will not participate.  Please keep us on your mailing list.

Please check the spaces below

(  ) Varsity Large School - 1200 and over enrollment     (  ) JV will participate

(  ) Varsity Small School - Below 1200 enrollment         (  ) JV will not participate
```

Figure A.2. Response card

rules and information sheet. Figures A.3 and A.4 show a sample confirmation letter and a sample information sheet, respectively.

Rules and Information

Include a list of rules and other information in the confirmation packet. For example:

- The home team will be determined by a coin toss, with the team traveling the greatest distance calling the toss, except for playoff rounds where the higher placed team will be the home team. If both teams placed the same, then revert back to the coin toss.

- The home team will be the official scorekeeper and will be responsible for submitting the score summary sheet to the snack bar, who will in turn be calling the line scores to the local newspaper. The visiting team will be responsible for the operation of the scoreboard.

- All games, except the championship game, will have a one hour and 30 minute time limit. No new inning will start after time has run out, unless the game is tied. If time has expired before the inning is over, you will be allowed to finish the inning. In the championship game, the tiebreaker rule will be in effect after 10 innings. The runner will start at second base each inning.

- The tournament tiebreaker rule will be in effect in the eighth inning if the game is tied. The tiebreaker rule will also be in effect with the start of the new inning if the time has run out before seven complete innings could be played and the score is tied. The last out of the previous inning will start the inning at third base.

- Each team will furnish one ball each game. The home team will furnish one new ball and the visiting team will furnish one good used ball. The plate umpire must accept the used ball. The

```
SAMPLE CONFIRMATION LETTER

January 22, 2003

Dear Softball Coach,

We have received your response card and entry fee for the 2004 Easter Softball
Classic hosted by Clovis High School and Katy High School.  We have your team
entered at this time.  The dates for this year's tournament are April 3rd, 5th, and
6th.  You will receive your tournament information packet and bracket sheets in
early March.  If you have any questions, you may call me anytime.

Thanks,

Mike Noel, Clovis Softball
(H)  (559) 555-1212
(W)  (559) 555-1213
```

Figure A.3. Confirmation letter

Easter Softball Classic
Information Sheet

School Name: ______________________ Coach: ______________

School Colors: ____________________ Dist/Class: ______________

No.	Name	Position	Class	Ht.
__	______________	_____________	_______	____
__	______________	_____________	_______	____
__	______________	_____________	_______	____
__	______________	_____________	_______	____
__	______________	_____________	_______	____
__	______________	_____________	_______	____
__	______________	_____________	_______	____
__	______________	_____________	_______	____
__	______________	_____________	_______	____
__	______________	_____________	_______	____
__	______________	_____________	_______	____
__	______________	_____________	_______	____
__	______________	_____________	_______	____

Figure A.4. Information sheet

only ball that will be used for this tournament is the yellow Dudley CFP-12.

- Forfeit time is game time. In the event of a forfeit, the team not forfeiting will receive a win and their runs for the tournament will be averaged at the end of pool play to determine a run total. A total of zero runs will be added to their runs allowed.
- Pool play winners and places will be determined by the following criteria:

  1st: Win-loss record

  2nd: Head-to-head competition

  3rd: Fewest runs allowed

  4th: Most runs scored

  5th: Coin flip

In the case of more than two teams ending pool play tied, once a winner of the pool has been decided using this criteria, the remaining teams will start back at criteria two to decide the second place team.

- A snack bar will be available throughout the entire tournament.
- Hitting any type of ball against any fence is not allowed.
- No warm-up on the infield will be allowed. If the game before yours has been completed, you may warm up in the outfield area. In addition, an area will be designated for warm-ups. As a safety precaution, throwing/warming up inside the complex between fields is not allowed.
- The umpires will start the game at the exact starting time according to the schedule.
- A trainer will not be on duty at the tournament.
- Two umpires will be assigned to each varsity game and one umpire to each junior varsity game. If for some reason umpires do not show by game time, then it might be necessary to reassign umpires so that each game has at least one umpire.
- Each team must furnish a roster of no more than 18 players and three coaches. This roster can be mailed ahead of time or turned in at the front gate upon arrival.
- Daily spectator admission cost is $4.00 per person and $2.00 for high school students with I.D. cards. Children under six years of age are free. An adult must accompany all children.
- Absolutely no liquor, smoking, or ice chests. Head coaches may bring in an ice chest for team use.

- Please clear dugouts quickly and hold team meetings outside the dugout area. Please pick up after yourself in the dugout areas and around the complex.

- In case of rain, the tournament will be postponed and completed during spring break. Please call the tournament director on the morning of a rainy day to find out if play has been cancelled.

- Individual and team awards will be given to the first and second place teams.

- Please park all buses in the designated area.

- The team on the left of the schedule will occupy the third base dugout, unless occupied from the previous game.

Tournament Formats

At a minimum, try to get at least eight teams to participate in the tournament, and construct a bracket similar to the one illustrated in Figure A.5. Figure A.5 shows the standard bracket most people use for an eight-team tournament. It can even be used with seven teams, with one team getting a bye.

If you have the facilities and the time, pool play is a great choice for a tournament format. Twenty-four teams can compete in four pools of six teams (Pool A, Pool B, Pool C, and Pool D). The winner of each pool is then entered into a four-team bracket (semi-finals and then the finals). This format guarantees teams at least five games, with an opportunity to play as many as seven. Figure A.6 is a sample tournament schedule using pool play with 24 teams.

One Month Before the Tournament

- Schedule umpires.

- Order awards.

- Order or make programs.

- Find a gatekeeper.

Scheduling Umpires

Schedule two umpires per field if possible, but one will do if you need to save money. Choose the best

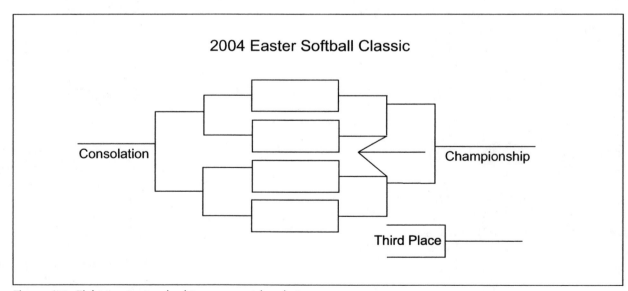

Figure A.5. Eight-team standard tournament bracket

```
                    EASTER SOFTBALL CLASSIC
                    VARSITY - LARGE SCHOOL
                            2003

            A              B            C            D
    1. Bakersfield   7. Buchanan   13. Bullard    19. Clovis West
    2. Madera        8. Centennial 14. Lemoore    20. Hoover
    3. Clovis        9. Hanford    15. Clovis East 21. Reedley
    4. Douglas      10. Highland   16. Monache    22. Delano
    5. Garrison     11. Central    17. Redwood    23. Liberty
    6. Porterville  12. Mt. Whitney 18. Stockdale 24. Hanford
```

	Saturday			Monday			Tuesday	
Field	Time	Game	Field	Time	Game	Field	Time	Game
2	9:00	13 v 15	2	9:00	15 v 16	2	9:00	13 v 16
3	9:00	9 v 12	3	9:00	7 v 11	3	9:00	7 v 9
4	9:00	3 v 2	4	9:00	2 v 4	4	9:00	3 v 4
5	9:00	22 v 24	5	9:00	19 v 24	5	9:00	21 v 24
2	11:00	13 v 17	2	11:00	14 v 15	2	11:00	15 v 18
3	11:00	11 v 12	3	11:00	7 v 12	3	11:00	8 v 12
4	11:00	3 v 1	4	11:00	2 v 6	4	11:00	1 v 6
5	11:00	20 v 22	5	11:00	19 v 22	5	11:00	19 v 20
2	1:00	15 v 17	2	1:00	16 v 17	2	1:00	14 v 17
3	1:00	9 v 11	3	1:00	8 v 11	3	1:00	10 v 11
4	1:00	1 v 2	4	1:00	1 v 4	4	1:00	2 v 5
5	1:00	20 v 24	5	1:00	23 v 24	5	1:00	22 v 23
2	3:00	14 v 18	2	3:00	13 v 14	2	3:00	1st C v 2nd D
3	3:00	7 v 8	3	3:00	10 v 12	3	3:00	1st B v 2nd A
4	3:00	5 v 6	4	3:00	3 v 6	4	3:00	1st A v 2nd B
5	3:00	19 v 23	5	3:00	21 v 22	5	3:00	1st D v 2nd C
2	5:00	16 v 18	2	5:00	17 v 18			
3	5:00	8 v 10	3	5:00	8 v 9	3	5:00	Fd 2 v Fd 4
4	5:00	4 v 6	4	5:00	1 v 5	4	5:00	Fd 3 v Fd 5
5	5:00	21 v 23	5	5:00	20 v 23			
2	7:00	14 v 16	2	7:00	13 v 18	3	7:00	Finals
3	7:00	7 v 10	3	7:00	9 v 10			
4	7:00	4 v 5	4	7:00	3 v 5			
5	7:00	19 v 21	5	7:00	20 v 21			

Figure A.6. Twenty-four team pool play bracket

three umpires for the championship game, based on their performance in the early games.

Ordering Awards

Ask your athletic director for suggestions on a company to order awards from. You will need to order the following:

- First-place team trophy
- Second-place team trophy
- Consolation trophy
- Individual trophies for champions (optional)
- All-Tournament trophies (however many you decide, but eight to ten are plenty)
- MVP award
- Outstanding Coach award

Ordering or Making Programs

You can either have the programs printed by an outside company or do them yourself. With the scanners and computers that are currently available, you can make a pretty nice program yourself. If you

32nd Annual
Easter Softball Classic

April 3rd, 5th, and 6th

School Logo Here

Figure A.7. Cover for program

want to save some money, do it yourself. It doesn't have to be elaborate. Most people just want to see their kid's name and number in print.

Decide on a cover. Figure A.7 shows a sample program cover that could be used.

Type an appreciation to go on the inside cover. It could say something similar to the sample text shown in Figure A.8.

*Include the tournament results from the previous year on another pag*e. See Figure A.9.

Get all of the information sheets from each coach and get them typed. If one team doesn't send you

Sample Appreciation for Program

The Lady Cougars take this opportunity to express our appreciation to the many people who help make our tournament possible. Our sincere appreciation and thanks to the following members of the athletic department: Jody Jordan, Athletic Director; Coaches Michelle Noel, Tony Peterson, Josh Peterson, Grover Talbert, Tom Gerber, David Martell, Roger Scott and Trevor White for their time and effort to have a successful tournament.

In this our 32nd annual tournament, we wish to welcome the following teams, coaches, managers and fans to Clovis High School: Brazos, Montgomery, Hempstead, RTC, Boling, and Rockdale.

A coaches lounge with refreshments will be provided. We would ask the teams and fans not to take food or drinks into the complex. Thank you for your consideration of our building and facilities and we hope you enjoy the tournament.

Figure A.8. Appreciation for program

2004 Easter Softball Classic Results

CHAMPIONSHIP GAME: Clovis beats Tomball, 8-2
THIRD PLACE: Montgomery beats Giddings, 3-1
CONSOLATION: Sealy beats Hempstead, 4-3

ALL TOURNAMENT TEAM

Most Valuable Player: Rebekah Jordan, Bellville
Winning Coach: Mike Noel

Norma White, Clovis	Denita Young, Clovis
Ramey Beard, Clovis	Wegi Talbert, Brazos
Vicki Beard, Montgomery	Sandra Talbert, Hempstead
Cheryl Martell, Sealy	Lisa Peterson, Tomball
Michelle Noel, Tomball	Laurie Adair, Tomball

Figure A.9. Tournament results

the information sheet, call them and have them fax you one. If they don't get you one on time, they just miss out. As a general rule, allow one page per team. In fact, you can combine several teams on one sheet if you are short on paper or funds. Figure A.10 shows a sample roster.

Take a copy of the tournament bracket and reduce it to fit in the program.

You can make the program with legal-size paper (8 x 14). Cut and paste your copies onto the legal-size sheets. You will need eight sheets to begin. Figure A.11 illustrates a sample eight-sheet program layout.

2004 Clovis Cougars

No.	Name	Class	Position
4	Jann Walther	Soph.	IF
5	Juliet Douglas	Senior	IF
7	Patricia Marek	Junior	OF
9	Irene Wilson	Soph.	P
10	Jennifer Beisel	Junior	OF
12	Norma White	Senior	C
14	Taylor Petersen	Junior	IF
20	Ronda Norman	Soph.	C
21	Cindy Pilcik	Soph.	DH
22	Carleen Noel	Junior	IF
25	Peggy White	Soph.	OF
27	Samantha Peterson	Senior	OF
32	Claire Scott	Senior	IF

Head Coach: Mike Noel
Assistants: Tim Douglas, Leland Grigsby
Manager: Josh Petersen

Figure A.10. Sample roster

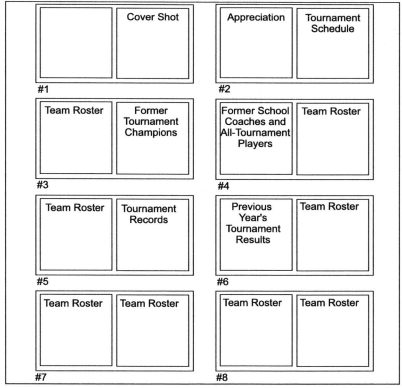

Figure A.11. Sample eight-sheet layout

Page two should be copied onto the back of page one. Page four should be copied onto the back of page three and so on. Once you have made your two-sided copies, place page seven/eight on top of page five/six and so on. Then fold the pages in half, and you have your program. If you have a heavy-duty stapler, you can staple in the fold to keep it all together. If this is your first year to run a tournament or you don't have records of previous tournaments, Figure A.12 shows a basic program outline.

Finding a Gatekeeper

Your school may have someone who usually keeps the gate for the regular season softball games. If you don't have a regular gatekeeper, or that person isn't willing to sit for that long, then add that responsibility to your clock and book assignment list.

Two Weeks Before the Tournament

Hospitality Room Sign-ups

Have your athletes sign up to bring something for a hospitality room, and then check to make sure you don't end up with too many desserts vs. real food.

You will probably want to purchase cups and canned drinks (using tournament-fee money), but check to see if you can get them donated.

One Week Before the Tournament

- Make a large bracket to post.
- Make packets for coaches.
- Assemble gift baskets (including seeds and gum) for dugouts.
- Order a sandwich tray for the hospitality room.
- Send information to the local paper.

Making Packets for Coaches

The packets for each coach should include the following:

- Letter to the coach (Figure A.13)
- All-Tournament ballots (Figure A.14)
- A tournament bracket for the coach
- Programs for players and coaches
- Rules and information sheet

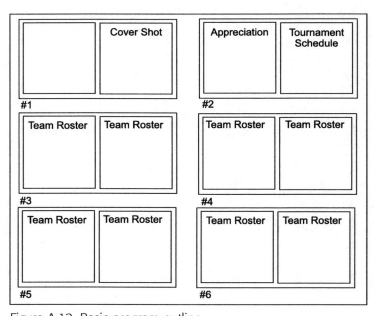

Figure A.12. Basic program outline

```
Sample Letter to Coaches


Welcome to the Easter Softball Classic.  We hope that you enjoy the tournament
and will return next year.

Enclosed you will find the following items:
        All-Tournament Ballots
        Tournament Schedule
        Rules and Information Sheet
        Programs for players and coaches

At the completion of each game, please fill out the All-Tournament Selection Ballot
and give it to Stephenie Jordan.  Don't forget to visit the coaches/officials
hospitality room located behind the concession stand.

If you need anything, please let me know.
```

Figure A.13. Letter to coach

```
                        Easter Softball Classic
                        All-Tournament Ballot


Nominate two players from your team and two players from the opponents team.
Just indicate by the player's number.

Nominating Coach: _____

Name of your team: _____    Opponent's Team: _____

            1. _____                      1. _____

            2. _____                      2. _____
```

Figure A.14. All-Tournament ballot

Sending Information to the Local Paper

Send your local newspaper any pre-tournament information that can be printed for a story (e.g., favored team, outstanding players, outstanding coaches, or any other information). A finalized tournament schedule should also be included.

The Day Before the Tournament

• Remind all athletes to bring food for the hospitality room.

• Buy cups, napkins, utensils, plates, and canned drinks.

• Prepare the ice chests.

• Put reminders in coaches' boxes for times they work.

• Make out an excuse list for your team if they play before school is out.

• Prepare the scorebook to be used as the official book.

• Pick up the sandwich tray.

• Set up the field.

The Day of the Tournament

• Make coffee for the hospitality room.

• Get ice and cover drinks in coolers.

- Make sure the dressing rooms and dugouts are clean.
- Set up the hospitality room as athletes bring food.
- Give programs to the gatekeeper.
- Give coaches the information packets as they arrive, and direct them to the dressing rooms.
- Have pencils ready for the scorebook.
- Set up the scoreboard.

After each trophy game, hand the coach their trophy and get ready for the next game. It doesn't have to be a big production unless you want it to be. All-Tournament selections should be announced at the conclusion of the championship game. Be sure to clean the dressing rooms and dugouts and take care of the food in the hospitality room.

After the Tournament

- Report results to the newspaper.

- Send a final letter to coaches.
- Send thank-you notes to helpers.

Reporting Results to the Newspaper

Fax or call in the tournament results to your local paper as soon as the tournament ends. Include the MVP, tournament champions, etc. The sportswriter will ask you what he wants to include in the results.

Sending a Final Letter to Coaches

Send a letter to each coach who participated in the tournament and include the final results of the tournament. See Figure A.15 for an example.

Sending Thank-you Notes to Helpers

Figure A.16 shows an example of a letter of appreciation that could be sent to those individuals who helped run the tournament.

Sample Final Letter to Coaches

Dear Coach,

We hope you enjoyed the Easter Softball Classic and hope you will plan to attend next year. Please feel free to give us feedback on how we can improve the tournament for next year.

Enclosed are the tournament results. The Clovis coaching staff hopes you are successful this season and look forward to hearing from you in the spring when we begin planning next year's tournament.

Sincerely, Mike Noel

Figure A.15. Final results letter

Sample Letter of Appreciation

To:

From: Coach Jordan

The Cougar Softball Team and I would like to express our appreciation to you for your help and support during the tournament. Your efforts were a big part of making our tournament a success.

Sincerely,

Stephenie Jordan

Figure A.16. Sample letter of appreciation

Field Maintenance

Turf Maintenance

Fertilization

Fertilizing is the most important part of turf maintenance and should be done at four times throughout the year: winter, summer, after overseeding, and during the season.

- Winter – use 22-10-4.
- Summer – use 12-12-12.
- After overseeding – use 6-20-20 XB.
- During the season – use 16-6-8. During the season, apply the fertilizer every six weeks.

Weed Control

By using a pre-emergent, such as Surflan, you can eliminate a lot of extra work during the season. Apply a pre-emergent twice a year, once in the fall and again in the spring. Another helpful application, such as Bueno 6, should be used twice a year to prevent broad leaf weeds.

Watering (Irrigation)

Watering should be done as needed. Watering should always be done in the early morning, around 4 a.m., to eliminate the chances for a fungus to develop.

Top Dressing

Top dressing, which is applying a fine sand to any low spots on the turf, allows for a safer and more true playing surface. Top dressing can be done three times a year. Including a top dressing schedule in the fall, spring, and summer will also help with the irrigation of the field.

Overseeding

Overseeding, which is done around October, helps keep the turf green year-round. By applying a perennial rye grass, you'll have a plush green playing surface to start the season instead of dormant Bermuda.

Mowing

Mowing is a vital part of maintaining a safe, good-looking playing turf. You should mow as necessary. Length is a personal preference, but you should never cut too much during one cutting.

Non-turf Maintenance

Skinned Infield

The most user-friendly infield surface material is crushed brick. It is easily maintained and provides a great-looking reddish-brown color. For an even better playing surface, a clay/brick mixture is your best option. This mixture allows for the same great color and ease as the crushed brick, but also allows for a better playing surface. Any infield surface with a clay mixture will demand extra attention. Nail dragging and watering must be done on a regular basis to avoid the material becoming hard and too compacted.

Pitcher's Circle

The pitching circle is one of the most abused areas of the field. It is important that special care be given to this area. A heavy clay product should be used in all the landing points of the circle. All holes should be filled on a daily basis and, if possible, a mat should be placed there during practice and when the field is not in use. The mat will reduce any holes that will be formed, as well as keep the area moist so that the clay product will not dry out.

Home Plate Area and Bullpens

The home plate area is also a very abused area. It's important that special care also be given to this area. A heavy clay product should be used in both batter's boxes, as well as the catcher's area. All holes should be filled on a daily basis and, if possible, a mat should be placed there during practice and when the field is not in use to reduce any holes that will be formed, and to keep the areas moist so that the clay product will not dry out.

Warning Track

A warning track is an important part of any field. It provides for both a safer and more attractive playing area. The warning track should be about 10 to 15 feet wide and any material, such as crushed brick, deposed granite, or just dirt, can be used. The key is that the athletes feel a difference when they reach the track. The warning track can easily be maintained by dragging it on a weekly basis.

Photo: David Menedian

136

C

Fundraising Ideas

If your program needs a few things, but you don't have enough money in the budget, you can arrange a fundraiser and generate up to $1000 per event. You can always resort to bake sales and car washes, or use one of the ideas presented in this section.

Powder Puff Football Game

Powder puff is a flag-football game played by the girls during the last few weeks of school against your rival school. The game is played exactly like a regular Friday night game (officials, announcer, down markers, etc.) and coached by varsity football players. You can even have a pep rally that day with male cheerleaders. If you can get your school's band to attend the game, it makes it an even better event. You need to get started by the first of May (or even sooner) if you want it to work.

How to Get Started

- Talk to your principal and get approval.
- Check with the football coach for use of the field.

- Have your principal call the opponent's principal and get a contact name.
- Put the date on the school calendar so it doesn't conflict with anything else.
- Have varsity boys sign up to coach or be cheerleaders.
- Have girls sign up to play.
- Check with PE teacher for football flags.
- Organize the concession stand.
- Arrange a time to meet with the other sponsor.
- Talk to the cheerleading sponsor and the cheerleaders.

Finding a Sponsor

The most difficult task may be finding someone from the other school to agree to sponsor such an event. After clearing it with your principal, call the principal from the other school and find out if they are interested in participating. If the other school's principal thinks it's a good idea, you can work together to find someone to sponsor the game, and you can go from there. If football is a big deal in your area, you can assure potential sponsors that they can make at least $800 to $1000, and even more if they have a concession stand.

Sign-up Day

Once everyone is in agreement (including the athletic director and head football coach), have a sign-up for varsity football players who want to coach. Once you've seen who has signed up, you can delegate who you want to be the head coach. He can then choose who he wants as his defensive coordinator, special teams coordinator, etc. You should also have a sign-up for cheerleaders. Let them know that they will be wearing skirts, wigs, and make-up and will perform a short dance at halftime (more on cheerleaders later). You will also need three people to take care of the down markers. You may or may not have to coax your girls into playing. Have them sign up, and if your best athletes aren't planning to play, find a way so they will! Be sure to make a team roster to hand out at the games once you've decided on positions.

Flags for the Game

Check with your physical education teachers for flag-football flags. You should have enough for *both* teams to use. See the rules section for guidelines on how to wear the flags properly.

Concessions

The most stress-free way to provide the fans with a concession stand is to let the pros take care of it. Whoever traditionally does the concessions at regular home football games would be your best bet. Call whoever is in charge and find out if they'll do it. They usually agree, but if not, check with another group in the school who'd like to do it (e.g., student clubs, athletic boosters, student council).

Meeting with the Other Sponsor

You'll need to meet with representatives of the other team to finalize rules and give them some flags to

practice with. Be sure to count the flags you've given out so you get them all back. A set of rules needs to be agreed upon by both parties. (Refer to the sample set of rules that is included in the next section of this appendix). The game is designed to be an 11-on-11 game with kickoffs, returns, field goals, etc., which are not normally included in a traditional flag football game.

❑ Flag Football Rules

The playing rules for the powder puff football game are the same as those used for a regular high school game with the following exceptions:

- Rushing the kicker on an extra point attempt or a punt attempt is not allowed.

- A punted ball will be dead where it touches the ground, but not on a kickoff.

- All players of the offensive team are eligible receivers.

- Offensive blockers must have their hands clasped in front, as if setting a screen.

- Defensive players are not allowed to push or pull offensive players.

- Defensive players may not hold a ball carrier in order to grab the flag.

- A player is considered down when her flag is pulled or if a flag falls off while in play.

Keep the following equipment guidelines in mind:

- Shirts or jerseys must be tucked in so flags are clearly visible and accessible.

- Both teams will use a junior high football.

- Soccer-type cleats may be worn and are recommended.

- Both teams will agree on the type of flags to be worn.

Meet with the Cheerleaders

Have the cheerleaders take your group of boys who bravely signed up and transform them into polished cheerleaders. They should learn at least three cheers and a short dance routine for the pep rally and halftime show. Let your real cheerleaders do all of the planning for the pep rally (signs, introductions of players, etc.) and for the game. The football girls will need a sign to run through, too, as they come onto the field. The boys are really the highlight of the whole game, so be sure they are dressed accordingly (e.g., wigs, makeup). Instead of trying to stuff big guys into cheerleading tops, have them wear their football jerseys with cheerleading skirts so everyone knows who they are.

Organizing Practice

Saturday afternoons are really the best times to get everyone there for practice. You'll have to be present at all practices, of course. You'll need to give the individual who is serving as your head coach some direction on what to do during practice and who to play. Consider yourself the Jerry Jones of the entire operation since you want to win and you don't want anyone to be embarrassed on the field. That's not to say the coaches aren't competent, but since you had the training to be a coach, you should help. Once the game starts, however, let them call the plays. Just help with personnel decisions and practice organization.

Personnel Decisions

• Find a quarterback. You will be most successful if you have someone who can throw the ball well. Use junior high footballs since they are smaller and easier to handle. The main emphasis of your offense should be passing the ball and using misdirection plays (e.g., reverses), but more on that later.

• Find out who can catch the ball. Get someone who can throw the ball (your newly found quarterback if possible), line up the players, and have them run routes as illustrated in Figure C.1. Throw three to five passes at each route and have one of the coaches keep track of who makes a catch. Specify routes; some girls might catch an easy short slant pass but have trouble with the long ball (if you have a quarterback that can throw the long ball, that is).

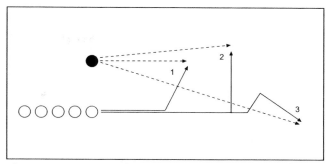

Figure C.1. Suggested passing routes

• Find a center. You have to find someone who can snap the ball to the quarterback in a shotgun formation and then immediately block the player in front of her.

• Make your fastest four or five players your running backs. Since your running backs will not run right through the line in too many instances, you want quickness to run sweeps and reverses.

• Put anyone who is aggressive and not afraid of contact on the line (defensive and offensive). The line is usually a place for your slower girls to play and do well.

• Find a place kicker and punter. Ask who wants to try out for these positions and have them work with a coach. They might need some instruction from your varsity kicker and punter on technique, but usually you have a young woman who can just do it naturally.

• Put the rest of your players on special teams. If some players who want to be involved are not that talented at football, then they can be on the kick and kick return team or the punt and punt return team. They can also practice as back-up o-line and d-line players. You want to let everyone contribute—and still beat the dog out of the other team.

• Determine who will be your linebackers and secondary players. Linebackers stand just behind the defensive line and stop running backs, quarterbacks, and tight ends. The secondary players cover the receivers on pass plays and serve as the last line of defense on running plays. Because linebackers are generally quick players, use your running backs and quarterback in these positions. A common defense uses three linebackers (i.e., a 4-3) but your boys' team might do something different. Players in the secondary need to be quick as well, but should know how to play man-to-man coverage. Your coaches will tell them what to do.

Drills for Practice

The first practice should be spent finding the right people for each position. After that first day, each young woman should know what position she primarily plays. As a result, when you start practice, everyone knows which coach to report to. The following drills are recommended, although your coaches could and probably will add others that they think would be effective.

❏ Running Backs

Ball exchange drill—Players form two lines facing each other about six to eight yards apart; one player gets the ball. On command, the first player in each line starts running at the first player from the other line. When they meet, they execute an exchange of the ball, using the proper handoff technique. At that moment, the next player starts to get the next handoff, and then hands off the ball to the next player coming at her. Refer to Figure C.2.

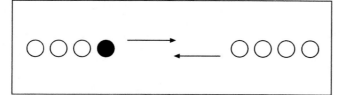

Figure C.2. Ball exchange drill

Pitch drill—Players line up in a normal position behind the quarterback. Precise positioning will be determined by specific plays designed by the coach. On a signal from the quarterback, the first player receives the pitch in proper position and continues across the line of scrimmage. Players get reps going both ways. Refer to Figure C.3.

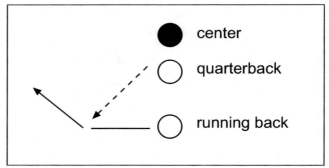

Figure C.3. Pitch drill

❏ Quarterbacks

Two-knee drill (20 passes)—Quarterbacks pair off about 10 yards apart, directly in line with each other, while both members of the pair are kneeling on both knees. The receiver will hold both of her hands up, giving the quarterback a target to throw to. Tell the players not to throw hard, and to concentrate on the target.

One-knee drill (20 passes)—The quarterback puts her throwing-side knee down. She places the ball on the ground, grips it with just the throwing hand, lifts it up with one hand, cocks it high with two hands, and throws to the drill partner. Players should exaggerate the follow-through.

Feet parallel drill (20 passes)—Players pair off 12 yards apart, directly in line with each other. They increase the distance as the drill continues. Tell the players not to exceed 20 yards, and not to step with the foot.

Circle toss (three minutes)—Players run in a circle, playing catch to simulate throwing on the run, then reverse the action.

Sprint out drill (20 passes)—Players sprint right and left. They throw to another quarterback or to a specific target, making sure shoulders and hips are square to the target.

Individual pass routes drill—Quarterbacks throw to a receiver running any of the individual pass routes. This drill is designed to teach timing.

□ Receivers

Quick ball drill—Players line up about 10 yards from the quarterback or coach. They run across the field at half speed, catch the ball, and then line up on the other side. The drill can be repeated several times with variations on passes: low balls, high balls, and balls thrown behind the player. Refer to Figure C.4.

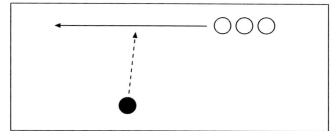

Figure C.4. Quick ball drill

Tap-dance drill—Players line up about 15 yards from the sideline. On command, the receiver starts to run three-quarter speed toward the sideline. The coach or quarterback will throw the ball about five yards from the sideline, and the receiver will catch the ball and plant one foot inbounds before going out. Use this drill on the left and right side. Refer to Figure C.5.

Turn-and-up drill—Use the same procedure described for the tap-dance drill, but in this drill the

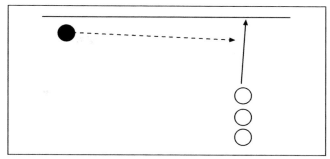

Figure C.5. Tap-dance drill

ball should be thrown seven to eight yards in front of the player so she can adjust and turn upfield. Refer to Figure C.6.

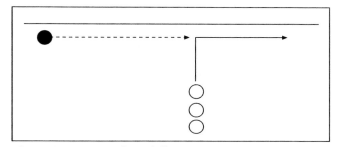

Figure C.6. Turn-and-up drill

Running routes—A universal wide receiver route tree that you can use to run individual routes is illustrated in Figure C.7.

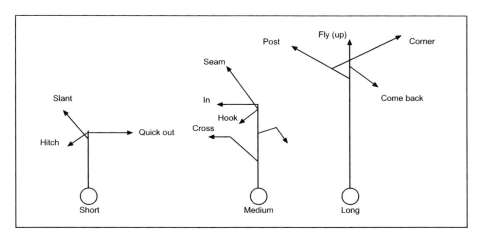

Figure C.7. Route-tree drill

❑ Defensive/Offensive Line

Playing on the line is tricky because the rules govern how much contact can be made, since no one is wearing pads or helmets. Both the offensive and defensive linemen should get down in at least a three-point stance and then come up with hands clasped in front of them, similar to setting a screen in basketball. This requirement needs to be the case for both teams, since the center has to get down to snap the ball. Otherwise, she is at a great disadvantage, having to come up and block someone who is already in a standing position. Your boys can teach the girls what to do: whom to block, where to block, etc., according to the play.

❑ Linebackers

Flag-grabbing drill—Players should form two lines in front of each other about 10 yards apart. All girls should be wearing flags. One player approaches the other, staying within a five-yard lane, while the other tries to grab the flag. Refer to Figure C.8.

Live-action drill—While running backs are running the pitch drill, the linebackers can practice grabbing the flags.

Secondary drill—While receivers run routes, the secondary can practice covering the receivers. Mix up routes.

The Playbook

Figures C.9 through C.14 illustrate a few plays that should work well. Any misdirection play you run should fool the defense, since most girls haven't been exposed to football very much. Also, passing the ball will be your best bet offensively if you've got the athletes to handle the demands of the passing game. Run these plays to the right or left.

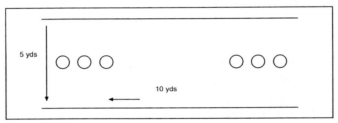

Figure C.8. Flag-grabbing drill

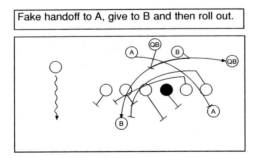

Fake handoff to A, give to B and then roll out.

Figure C.9. G.T. right

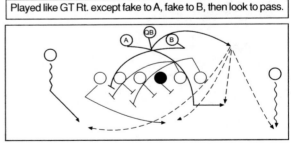

Played like GT Rt. except fake to A, fake to B, then look to pass.

Figure C.10. G.T. right pass

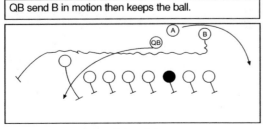

QB send B in motion then keeps the ball.

Figure C.11. Right, right, right.

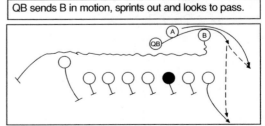

QB sends B in motion, sprints out and looks to pass.

Figure C.12. Right, right, right pass.

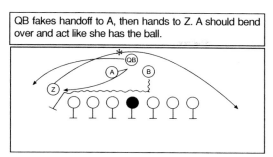

QB fakes handoff to A, then hands to Z. A should bend over and act like she has the ball.

Figure C.13. 48 sweep reverse.

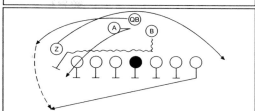

QB fakes handoff to A, fakes to Z, then rolls out for a pass.

Figure C.14. 48 sweep reverse pass.

Practice Outline

Practice #1

60 minutes   Tryouts for positions

Practice #2

30 minutes   Individual skills in groups (a player should rotate after 15 minutes if she is playing more than one position).

15 minutes   Extra point

15 minutes   Punt

Practice #3

20 minutes   Individual skills (rotate after 10 minutes if a girl is playing more than one position).

30 minutes   Offense (learn plays using note cards)

15 minutes   Punt return

Practice #4

30 minutes   Offense vs. second-team defense

20 minutes   Defense vs. second-team offense

15 minutes   Kickoff

Practice #5

30 minutes   Defense vs. second-team offense

20 minutes   Offense vs. second-team defense

15 minutes   Kick return

Practice #6

Scrimmage vs. freshman boys

You can obviously have more than six practices. If you have the time and energy then, by all means, increase the amount of time devoted to practicing. The kids really enjoy it and will be there no matter how many times you meet. Have the cheerleaders meet at the same time, so you don't have to go another time to cheerleading practices too.

Preparations for Game Day

- Make sure the band will attend.
- Confirm availability of the concession stand.
- Get officials for the game.
- Hand out jerseys.
- Have a team meeting (coaches, cheerleaders, players, helpers).
- Get the down markers ready.
- Get an announcer, and another person to videotape the game, including halftime.
- Publicize the event.

Band Attendance

If the band can attend, great! If not, make a tape of both the school song and the fight song and play it over the loudspeaker.

Officials for the Game

You may try scheduling junior high football officials and explain the rule changes. Or consider using intramural officials from a nearby university.

Jerseys for the Girls

The day before the game, you should hand out jerseys. Hopefully your athletic director or head coach will be cooperative. Try to accommodate your players' desires for numbers, but that is not always possible. Get the jerseys and hand them out starting with seniors, then juniors, etc. If your girls have workout shorts, they can wear them for the game so everyone looks the same.

The Big Meeting

Your coaches should dress alike for the game. It looks sharp and professional. Most of the time, varsity football players have a travel shirt they can wear with khaki pants. It just adds to the atmosphere. Have the coaches, cheerleaders, and powder puff players wear their outfits to the meeting and take pictures and then go over the game plan (when to be there, what to wear, etc.).

Publicity

Put ads in your local paper and post signs all over town to encourage attendance. Be sure to mention the cheerleaders, as some people will attend the game just to see male football players dressed as cheerleaders. Make announcements at school and post signs in the opposing school's town, too.

Golf Tournament

To a great degree, the amount of money you raise from this type of tournament depends on how much the golf course is going to charge you to let everyone play. When it's to benefit a program in the school, it doesn't really matter to some people how much it costs. A $50 fee should include the greens fee, cart, and awards. You can move the fee higher and add amenities, if you prefer. You could also sell mulligans for $5 each (limit four). Provide refreshments and give out T-shirts for all participants. The T-shirts are optional if funds won't allow the expense.

The format of the tournament should be a four-person scramble with a shotgun start (everyone starts at the same time but at different holes). Try to sign up at least 10 teams. You may have to limit the number of teams depending on how many carts the golf course will have available. Give awards to the first-, second-, and third-place teams. Individual awards should be presented for longest drive and closest to the hole. You can give certificates for other awards such as last-place team, slice king/queen, and slowest team. Make up more if you feel so inclined.

Eight Weeks Before the Tournament

- Call the golf course, strike a deal (carts included), and set a date.
- Publicize the tournament at both the course and around town.
- Send entry forms to potential golfers (see Figure C.15).
- Line up volunteer helpers.

Four Weeks Before the Tournament

- Order plaques and T-shirts.
- Ask businesses to help sponsor the tournament.
- Pay golf course required fees.

Order Plaques and T-shirts

The school may have someone it deals with for plaques and trophies. Ask your athletic director who it is or if he has any catalogues you might find useful. He also might have worked with a printer who will give you a relatively good deal on shirts.

Sponsors

You can earn more money by selling sponsorships for each hole. Charge $50 to the sponsor in exchange for a sign on that hole, advertisement, etc.

<table>
<tr><td colspan="2" align="center">**1st Annual Golf Tournament**</td></tr>
<tr><td>WHEN:</td><td>April 24th, shotgun start at 8:00 a.m.</td></tr>
<tr><td>WHERE:</td><td>Community Golf Course</td></tr>
<tr><td>FOR:</td><td>Taylor High School Girls' Athletics</td></tr>
<tr><td>COST:</td><td>$50 per person (includes cart, greens fee, "goodie bag," and awards)</td></tr>
<tr><td>PRIZES:</td><td>$200 first prize, four Wilson golf bags, $100 longest drive, $100 closest to the pin, and others</td></tr>
</table>

Mulligans available for purchase on the day of the tournament ($5 each — limit two per person).

Make checks payable to Anywhere H.S. and return the entry form and fee by March 30th to Coach Shaver.

Team captain: _____ Number: _____

Team members: _____

_____

_____

Entry fee: _____ (# indiv's X $50 each)

_____ (# of mulligans X $5 each)

Amount of $ enclosed: _____

Figure C.15. Entry form

One Week Before the Tournament

- Get drinks.
- Pick up T-shirts and plaques.
- Make "farthest drive" and "closest to the pin" markers.
- Make a poster to record all scores.

T-shirts

Put a nametag in each T-shirt, and then alphabetize the T-shirts to speed up handing them out.

Making the Markers

The markers should have a piece of paper with at least 10 lines for 10 names (more if the tournament is really large). Secure it to a piece of wire and stick it in the ground.

Scoreboard

Put team members' names in one column and leave a space for their score underneath. As each team finishes, record the scores on the board for everyone to see, as shown in Figure C.16.

John Smith Susan White Steve Scott Joe Garza	Sheryl Ham Lisa Porter Marge Frank Cindy Hall	Joseph Smith Danny Long Chris Lopez Al Johnson
72	69	75

Figure C.16. Scoreboard

The Big Day

- Ice down the drinks.
- Put out the markers and signs for hole sponsorship.
- Post the names of team members on carts, along with the specific hole where they will start play.
- Arrange the plaques on a table.
- Set up a table for purchasing extras and a table for registration.
- Meet with everyone at 7:50 a.m. to get organized.

Putting the Markers Out

Put the longest drive marker on a par-five hole that is somewhat wide open. The closest-to-the-hole marker should be placed on a short par three. Let teams know at the meeting which holes you've chosen.

Purchasing "Extras"

- Mulligans — limit four per person.
- Tiger Woods Drive — participants can purchase one automatic 250-yard drive.
- The String — a 12-inch long string to be used for assistance with short putts.

After the Tournament

Once every team has finished, send someone out to pick up the markers and gather everyone for the awards presentation. Depending on the number of people who will be involved in the awards presentation, it can be extremely informal. If it's a large gathering, you may want to seat everyone in the clubhouse and use a podium for the presentations. Be sure to clean up all trash and park the carts in the appropriate place afterwards.

Co-Ed Softball Tournament

Use the same format for the golf tournament, with the following changes:

- Get permission for use of the boys' baseball field.
- Go to neighboring towns and recreation centers to recruit teams.
- Charge at least $100 per team.
- Require each team to provide two softballs (check the size of the softballs).
- Hire three to four umpires.
- Get an official scorekeeper and clock/score-board keeper.
- Mail a bracket sheet to the coach in charge of each team.
- Organize a concession stand.
- Present T-shirts for the first-, second-, and third-place teams.

Using the Baseball Field

A baseball field is more appropriate than a softball field since it is a coed tournament. Technically, the fence should be between 275 feet and 300 feet, and the bases should be moved to 60 feet or 65 feet instead of 90 feet. The pitching distance should be 46 feet, using a 12-inch ball. The day before the tournament, mark the baseline/foul lines and the batter's box. Each side of the plate should be a 3' x 7' rectangle.

Recruiting Teams

Go to neighboring grocery stores and churches to publicize the tournament. If you live in a larger city, you may have a city softball league where you can solicit teams during their games. Post a flyer in each dugout, and you will have plenty of teams interested.

Getting Umpires

If your baseball and softball coaches are not participating in the tournament, you could ask them to call the games for you. If they are playing, you can do one of two things. Either call the recreation center in your city and ask them for some names of umpires that call city games, or call some umpires from the local baseball or softball chapter your school uses. Check to see what they usually earn for games and offer them the same level of compensation.

The Bracket

If you only have one field, it must have lights. The maximum number of teams you should allow is eight, which means a total of 11 games. Each game should have a time limit of 50 minutes, except the championship game. Each game is a seven-inning game with the normal run rule of 10 runs after five innings or 15 runs after four innings.

The Scorekeeper, Time Keeper, and Scoreboard Keeper

Three people or just one can do these jobs. A scoreboard is not necessary, but a neutral scorekeeper and someone to keep the time for each game is important. These jobs could be done by the coaches who are helping you put on the tournament, or you could pay people to fill these positions.

Concession Stand

If you can get someone to grill hamburgers, you can make quite a bit of additional money. Provide a meal of a hamburger, chips, and a drink for around $3.00. This idea will be especially successful if you are a small community without the convenience of a fast-food option. Have bottled water available as well.

T-Shirts

If possible, specify first, second, or third place on the shirts. Or, for convenience, you could print one design for all the T-shirts. Order at least 45 shirts (10 players and five subs per team).

Adhering to the Scheduled Time

Stay as close to the schedule as possible so that the teams know when they will play. However, make each team aware that if a game ends unusually early, the next game will start immediately. Allow 10 minutes for a team to show and then call it a forfeit.

Other Ideas

Garage sale—Use items donated by community members.

Spaghetti supper—Get merchants to donate ingredients and have the dinner before a home football game.

Potluck supper—Have parents of players bring dishes for the supper and have a set charge per plate. Seconds are allowed, but individuals are charged for another plate. Set up a silent auction with items such as old uniforms, cakes, pies, donated gifts from area merchants, season tickets to your home games, booster wear items, etc.

Road race—This event can be similar to a cross-country meet. Give participants T-shirts and prizes for winners in each age division (you decide on the age groups).

Baked potato supper—Again, try to get food donated and include different toppings such as chopped meat, nacho cheese, etc.

Baby-sitting service—Reserve the gym and advertise a Parents' Night Out some Friday or Saturday. Have the girls baby-sit from 6:00 to 11:00 p.m. and charge $10.00 per child.

Car wash—Consider selling tickets beforehand. You might generate more revenue this way.

Bake sale—To put a twist on this one, have the girls spend the night together cooking—an all-night baking party. You might want to check into using the school cafeteria or a church fellowship hall rather than someone's house.

"Meet the Team" dinner—Use any of the supper ideas listed previously and turn it into a "Meet the Team" dinner. Include a silent auction and a raffle, sell your team's booster wear, and sell advertising space on place mats.

About the Authors

Mike Noel is in his ninth season at the helm of the Clovis High School softball team. In his first eight years with the Cougars, Noel's teams have combined for a record of 264-48-3, a winning percentage of .849. During his tenure, Noel has coached 11 All-Americans, 17 All-State selections, and 23 All-Valley picks.

During his eight-year career, Noel has been named Valley Coach of the Year three times and League Coach of the Year six times. He was further honored after the 1996 and 1999 seasons by being named a head coach in the annual summer All-Star game. Noel's teams have been ranked second (three times), third (twice), fourth, eighth, and fourteenth in the state during his eight years as head coach.

Noel, an active member of the National Fastpitch Coaches Association, joined the Clovis High staff in 1992 as a math instructor and coach. In addition to his head softball coaching duties, he has coached football for five years and baseball for one year. Noel has been a featured speaker at numerous coaching clinics, including ones in Lake Tahoe, Southern California, Arizona, and San Francisco.

Noel graduated from Fresno State in 1991 with a degree in business administration. While attending FSU, he played both football and baseball for the Bulldogs and earned Big West athletic and academic honors.

Noel and his wife, Tiffany, have a daughter, Avery Elizabeth. They are also proud parents of their dachshund, Sadie.

Stephenie Jordan earned her Bachelor of Science degree in mathematics from Southwest Texas State University with a minor in physical education. There she earned varsity letters in volleyball and track and field and was a two-time Southland Conference Champion. As of 2002, she was still the school record-holder in the heptathlon. Before attending SWTSU, she was recruited to Western Illinois University as a freshman pentathlete/heptathlete and earned All-Conference honors in the javelin for the Gateway Collegiate Athletic Conference. She also earned a varsity letter for volleyball at WIU.

During her high school athletic career, Stephenie was a varsity letterman in volleyball, basketball, tennis, and track and field at O'Fallon Township High School. She qualified for the state track meet in the discus and 300m hurdles, played on the number one doubles team in tennis, and was Athlete of the Year in 1987.

She began her coaching career in the summer of 1991 at Camp Ozark, where she was the head coach for all team competitions and later became the girls' sports director in 1993. Her first teaching job was at Bellville Junior High School, in Bellville, Texas, where she coached 64 girls in seventh grade. The following two years, she assisted the varsity Brahmanette volleyball team to a 3A state title in 1993 and to the state finals in 1994. Also at Bellville, Stephenie was the JV volleyball coach, the JV basketball coach, an assistant varsity track coach, the JV cheerleading sponsor, and director of Fellowship of Christian Athletes. She was also the tournament director of the 47th Annual Basketball Tournament and helped supervise the Little Dribbler's program.

Stephenie next accepted a teaching and coaching position in Arp, Texas, where she was the head track coach when 14 of 16 girls qualified beyond the district meet. In addition, she assisted the volleyball team as they advanced to the area finals, coached the JV and freshman volleyball teams, and again sponsored the Fellowship of Christian Athletes.

The following year, Stephenie and her family moved to Garrison, Texas, where she became the first softball coach at Garrison High School. After starting the program, the team went 8-4 and played in the first round of the playoffs. She also coached the junior high girls' basketball teams, assisted the varsity team, was the boys' and girls' cross-country coach, acted as Little Dribbler's program coordinator for two years, coached two high jumpers to the regional finals, and also sponsored the Fellowship of Christian Athletes.

Stephenie and her husband, Jody, have a son, Scott Douglas, and a daughter, Rebekah. She is also the author of *Developing a Successful Girls' and Women's Basketball Program* and co-author of *Developing a Successful Volleyball Program*. She has temporarily given up full-time coaching to raise their family and pursue a home-based web design business.